DEDICATION

For **Julie** and **Alora Veronica** who fill my life with joy and laughter.

DRAMA GAMES

Drama and Group Activities for Leaders Working with People of All Ages and Abilities

SECOND EDITION

Bernie Warren

CAPTUS PRESS

in association with

Players Press/Empire Publishing Service

Drama Games: Drama and Group Activities for Leaders Working with People of All Ages and Abilities, 2nd Edition

Originally published by MENCAP, 1981
First Captus Press edition, 1989
Second edition, 1996

*Simultaneously published Canada, Australia and the United States.
Address all sales enquiries within Canada and the United Kingdom to Captus Press Inc.*

Canadian Cataloguing in Publication Data

Warren, Bernie, 1953–
    Drama games : drama and group activities for leaders working with people of all ages and abilities

2nd ed.
Includes index.
Previous ed. published under title: Drama games : a practical guide for leaders working with disabled people.

ISBN 1–895712–98–X (Captus Press)
ISBN 0–88734–681–2 (Empire Pub. Service)

1. Drama — Therapeutic use. 2. Games — Therapeutic use. 3. Mentally handicapped — Recreation. I. Title.

LC4611.W37 1996   793'.0196   C96–931046–3

Library of Congress Cataloging-in-Publication Data

Warren, Bernie, 1953–
    Drama games : drama and group activities for leaders working with people of all ages and abilities / Bernie Warren. — 2nd ed.
        p.   cm.
    Includes bibliographical references.
    ISBN 0–88734–681–2 (alk. paper)
    1. Drama — Therapeutic use. 2. Handicapped — Rehabilitation.
3. Acting.   4. Games.   I. Title.
RC489.P7W37 1996
616.89'1523 — dc20
                                                                96–9429
                                                                CIP

0 9 8 7 6 5 4 3
Printed and bound in Canada

TABLE OF CONTENTS

Practical Activities 25

At-A-Glance Guide to Games 28

Further Reading 83

PREFACE

This is actually the third edition of *Drama Games* (the second with Captus Press). Originally it was written as a brief pamphlet to help leaders running summer projects with 'mentally handicapped' people. Over the past twenty years the book has developed a life of its own and, if my correspondence is to be believed, has become a fast friend to many besides myself.

While much of the original material remains unchanged, this edition has been revised extensively to accommodate many of the suggestions received from students and others since the publication of the last edition. Some stylistic changes have been made to the layout and the language used to make the book more accessible. New material has been added to address the particular challenges of running sessions with people with specific 'disabilities,' and with integrated and intergenerational groups. The material on leadership has been extended to consider not only working beyond the first session of *Drama Games*, but also developing *Drama Games* sessions into drama 'proper' and theatre performance. To this end the games section has been expanded. Throughout I have tried to remain true to the original concept of an easy-to-use book, accessible to non-specialists interested in drama work with persons with a disability.

I hope that *Drama Games* continues to be a useful introduction — not only for my own students but also for the many others working with people of all ages and abilities who want to bring drama into their lives.

Bernie Warren, PhD
Professor
School of Dramatic Art
University of Windsor
Windsor, Ontario
Canada
April, 1996

ACKNOWLEDGEMENTS

Many people have helped in the development and evolution of this book over the last twenty years. To this end I want to thank the following people:

Bill Morris and Rob Watling and especially the late Bert Amies, M.B.E. for introducing me to Social Drama; Tony, Ian, Cathy and Eva who helped to get the project started; all the people who read the original manuscript in its various forms of completion, particularly Dennis Cartwright who did his best to correct my English; and Victoria Shennan at MENCAP who supported the work through the publication of the first edition.

I particularly want to thank: Mary Lou Bell for her excellent editorial support in compiling the first Captus edition; Randy Hoffman and all the people at Captus Press who continue to support *Drama Games*; my friend and colleague Tim Dunne for his permission to use material that we jointly compiled for the first Captus edition, which helped to make it a success; all the people who over the years have helped me clarify ideas and games contained in the current book, especially Reg Topping and Judy Gray Royka; my editorial team (Christopher Hickman, Kim Baker and especially Bel Wolker), who helped in the development of this edition; and, above all, my thanks go to Edna P. whose sense of humour continues to keep me relatively sane.

Drama Games

INTRODUCTION

Drama Games is intended as a practical introduction to drama, primarily for leaders working with people with a disability. However, the activities presented herein are of value to leaders working with people of a wide range of ages and abilities, and may be used with integrated and intergenerational groups. The emphasis throughout this book is on *enjoyable participation rather than outstanding performance*. Consequently, what is presented is not a definitive text but rather a simple practical introduction — the beginning of a story that readers continue for themselves.

One of the major reasons for revising *Drama Games* has been the constantly shifting use of terms to describe people with disabilities. As I am well aware, language often creates reality. I have tried to use terms related to *disability* and *handicap* in ways which are neutral and non-judgmental. The term 'disability' is used throughout to describe a condition which makes the completion of a task or tasks more difficult. A disability may be sensory, intellectual or physical in nature. I also spent a great deal of time pondering the alternatives before I settled, in the interest of linguistic simplicity, on the plural 'they' to denote either gender, even when this is not strictly grammatically correct. It is likely that I will not please everyone with my choices but I hope that my intentions, and the material, remain clear and accessible.

A FEW WORDS ABOUT DISABILITY

When I first arrived in Canada, a well-meaning colleague 'threw' me in a room with Keith Johnstone, telling each of us separately that, because we were English, we would have a great deal in

1

common. After a very tentative and difficult first few minutes, it became clear that we did have a lot in common. What we share is not simply being born in England — a mere accident of birth — but rather a 'warped' sense of humour and a games-based approach to actor training and theatrical performance. Our common philosophies and methodologies are based on similar experiences of poor performances in various theatres around the world. We both recognize that the *accident of birth* we share, while having an effect on our development as individuals, is not the sole determinant of our personalities; the same is true of cerebral palsy, Down's syndrome, and any other 'disabling' condition.

All of us, you and me included, have some form of disability, the effects of which may handicap us in the performance of one or more *specific* tasks: I may not be able to fix my car when it breaks down, John may not be able to tie his shoelace without help.

It is extremely rare that a disabling condition handicaps a person totally or prevents that person from participating in and enjoying drama at some level. However, it is very easy, especially when first starting out, to be guided by labels — to see people only in terms of the disability that 'links' them. This is misleading. Using words like 'mentally handicapped' can be useful as a form of 'shorthand' in day-to-day conversation but it reduces people to statistics. While it may be helpful to say that people with a developmental disability have a 'developmental delay' or some form of 'specific learning difficulty,' these terms and others like them are totally inadequate when it comes to conveying the range of each individual's needs and abilities.

Having said all this, people with similar conditions are still often brought together as a group to participate in drama sessions which are specifically labelled for them: drama for the disabled, drama with the blind, etc. Grouping people together in this way, on the basis of similar conditions, implies that they have similar needs and aspirations. It is important to bear in mind that no two people have exactly the same problems and, consequently, the range of responses to the same situation, even from individuals who have the same condition, can vary enormously (not to mention variation from day to day as well as from situation to situation). While some of us are more limited in certain respects than others, each of us is unique and has both the potential and the right to be a creative member of society.

DRAMA AND THEATRE

Most people tend to equate drama with theatre. However, there are subtle but important differences between the two. **Theatre** is a collective art. Theatre requires many people — actors, writers, designers, technicians, etc. — all working together in a period of

2

rehearsal and creative exploration towards a common goal. Whatever the benefits experienced by participants along the way, theatre is evaluated by how well the performance is communicated to its audience.

Drama is an individual pursuit undertaken within a social context. Defined by human action and interaction, drama is primarily concerned with what happens to participants while they are engaged in the activity. It is an extension of children's play and, like that play, is often free and spontaneous. Drama has no fixed end product, no right or wrong way of doing things. As a result, its effects, unlike theatre performances, are often unique and unrepeatable. Above all, dramatic experience is a very human activity — one that reaffirms the belief: "I exist. My life has meaning."

PLAY, GAMES AND DRAMA

Simply put, play is free and unrestricted while games have rules. These rules are usually agreed on by the group in advance and adhered to, sometimes religiously, by the game's players. Play and games both provide a context for fantasy experience and both are meant to be fun. While all mammals display spontaneous behaviour that we might describe as play, games are usually considered peculiar to human beings.

Drama games work is an extension of the use of exercises and games in teaching specific acting techniques. Many drama games evolved as adaptations of well-known party games, children's street games and Victorian parlour games. They encourage a sense of playfulness within a clearly-defined structure (all games have a beginning, a middle and an end). This structure enables an individual to participate at their own level of ability.

Drama games are related both to childhood play and to theatre. Like children's games, they are an extension of the dramatic play of childhood but they also use the basic structure of theatre. Although many drama games originated as a means of training professional actors, their usefulness has been extended beyond the theatre stage to a variety of therapeutic and educational arenas.

WHY USE DRAMA GAMES?

It may be helpful to know some reasons for using drama games with a group. Some of these are obvious — entertainment, personal contact and break from routine. Other, less obvious, implicit and explicit educational and therapeutic benefits of drama games include:

- enjoyment;
- social integration;

- body awareness and physical control;
- creativity and self-expression;
- cognitive skill development;
- observation; and
- accessibility.

Enjoyment

Drama games offer an opportunity for fun and pleasure. It is widely believed that pleasure, in moderation, not only is a potent medicine for alleviating psychological disturbance but also may act as an important motivational element — one that encourages people to participate and succeed in spite of a disability. In fact, to be in any way beneficial, drama must first and foremost be enjoyable.

Social integration

People with a developmental disability rarely play spontaneously, and many people with other disabilities are excluded for one reason or another from active participation in sports, the arts and other communal activities. This can lead to social isolation. Drama games provide opportunities for social interaction in a supportive, relaxed and enjoyable environment. People can be helped not only to play in a group but also to acquire the skills necessary to good social functioning — learning to accept and understand rules, control impulses, live within the accepted rules, etc.

Body awareness and physical control

For all people, the body is a primary means of expression. Involvement in drama games helps participants gain an understanding of their body schema and start to generate a positive but realistic body image. In addition, games can help improve physical dexterity and control. By engaging in enjoyable activities in a supportive environment, a participant can better utilize their body's resources to communicate their feelings, and achieve success in physical tasks.

Creativity and self-expression

When individuals participate in drama games, they are physically, mentally and emotionally active. This total involvement helps encourage imagination, spontaneity and even abstract thought. For example, once participants understand the rules, they may try to bend them or may even make up new ones.

Participation in drama games demands a suspension of disbelief. Participants must be willing to separate themselves from reality for the duration of the game. This is not only essential to the game's success but also to an understanding that "it's only a game." This factor can also be a powerful psychological cue, providing the safe

4

context within which participants feel secure enough to express themselves fully. In suspending disbelief, participants can become immersed in the dramatic activity and — as a result — can more easily express feelings, thoughts and attitudes.

Cognitive skill development

Memory, concentration, reflectivity, anticipation of consequences and problem-solving can all be developed through drama games. Drama games can be structured to incorporate specific aims or objectives — increasing levels of body awareness or impulse control, building cooperation and trust among peers within the group, etc. This can be particularly helpful to teachers working with children who have special educational needs.

Observation

As well as the many benefits for participants, drama games provide leaders with the opportunity to view individual interactions within a playful creative environment. The way an individual plays often reveals information concerning that person's ability to cope with new situations, and illuminates interpersonal relationships among individuals in the group. The insight gained during a session of drama games can be used in planning general and specific programmes for individual participants.

Accessibility

Finally, a valuable aspect of drama games is that participants require no special talent to take part. Leaders do not have to be drama specialists to use them. In addition, games often prove valuable when working with any individual who requires extra structure or guidance. Individual games can be used in isolation as 'ice breakers,' 'fillers,' or to enhance the teaching of a concept or idea. Two or more drama games can be linked together to form a lesson, workshop or activity session, the purpose of which may be educational, therapeutic or merely entertaining.

Leadership

PREPARING FOR YOUR FIRST SESSION

The relationship between a leader and the group is crucial to the success of a session of drama games. It is the leader's job to control the proceedings and make sure that everything runs smoothly. To the person leading for the first time, this can seem a daunting task. However, good preparation and the use of common sense should mean that you are faced with few major headaches.

You will probably find it useful to gain some training in drama games. Many excellent drama and drama games workshops are offered by universities, theatre associations and advocacy groups. Another good idea is to work as a volunteer for leaders experienced in running drama/drama games sessions. Also, when you start, you may find that working as a team benefits your development as a leader. You may even find that team leadership is a good way of running all your sessions.

Just as no two people are exactly alike, so it is true that no two leaders are the same. Ultimately, each of us has to find a style of leadership that suits us best. This style is shaped by, among other factors, our age, experience, training and disposition.

GETTING TO KNOW YOUR GROUP

The first thing to do as a leader is to get to know your group. Finding out about group members well in advance can often be helpful for planning purposes. At the very least, make a point of

6

trying to meet everyone involved in the group before beginning the session. Spend time talking informally in a relaxed social setting before embarking on a session of games. This can be as simple as arriving fifteen minutes early.

If you are unable to meet the group before the session, speak to someone who knows them well. Learn about the specific needs of each individual within your group. In particular, determine whether individuals can talk, move freely without help and see and hear clearly. If anyone has a problem with these basic skills, ask for clear practical information; e.g., Fred can walk with the aid of a walker or Susie can speak for herself but tends to repeat what you said.

Pay special attention to any significant medical problems. It is also useful to know if anyone is taking medication which makes them sleepy or limits their involvement. Information such as I.Q. or mental age may be worth noting but is usually of less relevance. Remember that some of the most valuable information, such as an individual's sense of humour or creativity, is not usually contained in formal reports.

Make sure you know what, if anything, is expected from you. Above all else the goals of your session should be clear in your mind. If you are unsure what is expected of you, discuss the 'boundaries' of your work with your supervisor. Remember that your work is probably best directed towards building confidence, trust and self-awareness, in the hope that participants will find it easier to cope with social situations, rather than towards attempting to 'solve' individual 'problems.'

WORKING WITH HELPERS

While many people with a disability are totally independent, some individuals are physically dependent on others. The degree of assistance that an individual requires depends on the nature and degree of their disability and the skills required to participate in a particular game. At certain times a player with a disability may benefit from the assistance of a helper. This helper can be a friend, a relative, a member of the professional staff or a volunteer. The helper should be:

- instructed that they should only assist when asked;
- encouraged not to make assumptions about a participant's needs or limitations; and
- reminded that it is best to focus on a participant's ability rather than the challenges they face.

The delicate relationship among the leader, helpers and group members is crucial to the success of a session of drama games.

It is often helpful to play the games with your group's helpers before you play them with the group as a whole. This helps prepare helpers for their role by familiarizing them with the games, and demonstrating that the games are fun and easily accessible.

In addition, remember that your helpers can provide valuable feedback on your leadership. Make time to listen to their comments. This feedback is particularly valuable for new group leaders.

CHOOSING A ROOM

Simply put, where you work affects *how* you work. However, all one really needs for drama games to take place is a group and a space.

If you are one of the lucky few who has some say in the choice of room in which your group meets, consider the following:

- Is the room familiar to your group? If so, is it liked or is it associated with unhappy experiences?
- If the room is unfamiliar, does it have a friendly atmosphere? (Peeling wallpaper tends to detract from the session!) You should plan to spend a little time on allowing your group to become familiar with the room, e.g., using a game such as **Four Walls, a Floor and a Ceiling** (see page 38).
- Can you adjust the room's temperature? A room that is too hot or too cold often distracts participants.
- Take note of any dangers in the room — sharp ends of tables, exposed electrical sockets, glass cabinets, etc. Before playing a game, make participants aware of any dangers that might affect their safety during the game.
- What flooring does the room have — carpet, linoleum, other? Does this prevent you from doing certain games?
- Does the room contain enough chairs, mats or other comfortable seating? Avoid deep and luxurious armchairs — participants may not want to leave them or may fall asleep!
- It is an advantage if the room's lights can be dimmed or blacked out as this provides the opportunity to change or control the atmosphere in the room. Some simple spotlights with coloured filters are also helpful, as players can be inspired by coloured light.
- Can you close out noise and avoid interruptions? Rooms used as a general thoroughfare or close to noisy heavy machinery make your job more difficult.

If possible, find a room large enough for active games but not so large that the more intimate games are lost in it. The ambience of the room is probably more important than its size. Endeavour to create a quiet and supportive working environment. Do remember, however, that an enjoyable session can be run in *any* room. Make the best of the conditions.

PLANNING THE SESSION

The process of planning drama games for people with special needs does not differ much from planning for anyone else. Although it may be tempting to take material straight from a book or some other source without adapting it, **to be successful you must plan for** *your* **group's capabilities**.

Find out about the capabilities, likes and dislikes of the individuals in your group.

Know what you hope to achieve. Is it your intention, for example to: a) simply provide an enjoyable experience? b) stimulate basic language skills? or c) develop social skills? Also, ask whether these aims match your groups needs.

Here are a few pointers:

- Plan activities that will work in the space provided.
- If you are working with helpers, make sure they know what you expect of them.
- Plan activities that are appropriate for your group. There is no point in using a highly verbal game with 'language-disabled' participants.
- Aim for activities that allow participants to experience success early. There is no sense in reinforcing a cycle of failure and underachievement.
- Try to keep the size of your group manageable. The exact size depends on the capabilities of your group. A good starting size is eight to twelve.
- Aim for activities that enable participants to support each other.
- Start with non-threatening activities that are rewarding. Use name games to open the first few sessions until participants are comfortable with each other and with you.
- Choose a variety of activities for the first sessions. Choosing games that require different skills allows you to determine the capabilities of the members of the group.
- Do not try to be too ambitious early on. Choose seven or eight activities suitable for your group. Chances are you will only play four or five of them but it's always good to have a few ideas in reserve.
- If you are using music or other resources, make sure everything is prepared beforehand.
- Try not to make the session too long. The optimum length depends on the group's size, the capabilities of the participants

and the frequency with which you meet. For a small group of six to eight people, thirty to forty-five minutes of activity is a good starting place, while for a group of twelve to sixteen, you will need longer — perhaps fifty to seventy minutes.

- Try to build some time for reflection and/or discussion into each session.

Above all, always remember that everyone is a unique individual. Each participant has their own strengths and weaknesses, likes and dislikes. Try to keep this in mind when planning and running any session.

STRUCTURING THE SESSION

A simple basic structure for a drama games session is:

1. warm-up or opening phase;
2. simple exercises;
3. development; and
4. closure.

Warm-up or opening phase

The purpose of this phase is to establish trust, interest and motivation within the group. Use simple activities to 'warm up' the imagination and body. Name games are important in this phase, particularly within groups.

It is important to remember that games used as warm-ups set the tone for the rest of the session: If the session is to be energetic, choose a physical warm-up game like **Rob's Little Finger Game** (page 35) under the heading, "Warm-Up Games — Physical/ Non-Verbal Games."

Simple exercises

This phase makes use of simple exercises to introduce basic ideas, themes or images. Activities are often undertaken by the group as a whole or by individuals supported by the rest of the group. Examples include **Bing Bong** on page 41 (directionality — under heading "Warm-Up Games — Vocal Games") and **Liar's Tag** on page 43 (under heading "Warm-Up Games — Creative/Group Games"). It is quite usual for these simple exercises to flow into the next phase, which is the development of the simple ideas.

Development

This phase is directly related to the purpose of the specific drama session and usually takes place in small groups, pairs, or with individual participants working on their own. For instance, if the leader's intention is to work on body awareness and position in space, this phase might include games which focus on right/left discrimination and movement. Examples of appropriate games are **Tick** on page 53 and **Bombs Away** on page 54 (both under heading "Physical/High Energy Games").

Closure

As a session nears its end, it is important for participants to come down from whatever 'high' they may be on. This phase also provides the opportunity to bring the group together again. Examples of activities to use during this phase include **Relaxation** (page 66, under heading "Body Awareness, Trust and Sensitivity Games"), group discussion about the session, or a simple **Group Back Massage** (page 66, under the same heading).

RUNNING THE SESSION

Unfortunately, no one can tell you exactly how to run a session. Each leader has to find the approach that suits them best, and each approach is shaped by many factors, including age, familiarity with the group, training and experience. What I offer here are some useful hints.

First get the group's attention. Allowing a few minutes for the group to settle down before beginning the session makes this easier.

Maintaining each participant's attention throughout the session is critical, particularly when explaining the rules of each game. It is helpful to establish ways of holding attention. Possibilities include using simple command words (Listen! Watch! Stop!), sound (beating a tambourine), or a silent but clearly understood gesture (raising a hand above your head).

Always begin the first session with a name game.

Go slowly. Explain everything clearly, backing up verbal explanations with visual reinforcement. Try to include a practise run for each game so that participants know what is required.

If helpers are present ask them to place themselves among the group so they can easily assist other players if necessary.

Try to be flexible. Do not stick rigidly to the rules. If the rules are proving too difficult, simplify them. You may end up with a totally different game but one that works more effectively. If you do change the rules make sure everyone, particularly the helpers, understand the changes.

As the leader, it is up to you to assess how each game is working. You must decide when it's time for the next game. Don't worry — it is usually obvious when the group needs a change. Remember, not all participants will enjoy all games.

11

Be sensitive to the needs of the individuals in the group. Do not force an individual to play — let them sit and watch. Then, before the next game, ask how they feel and suggest joining in. Some individuals need more persuading then others.

Always be aware of those participants who might feel left out and those who need extra attention. In addition, take special care that the helpers do not overshadow the other players.

Remember, the helpers are a resource for you. Discuss how things went during the first session. See if they noticed things you did not. Ask them for any suggestions. When appropriate, follow up other sessions with similar discussions.

If possible, schedule the second session soon after the first so that memories of the first session are still fresh. Begin the next session with a name game and try to repeat one or two games that worked well in the first session. Do not worry if you only play two or three new games.

FIRST STEPS: COMMON CONCERNS, CHALLENGES AND PROBLEMS

When first setting out on their journey, people leading sessions of drama games often encounter similar problems.

Trying to do too much

First-time leaders often overplan. This is usually caused by anxiety about 'drying up' — that is, not having enough games to keep the session going. Tim Dunne recounts how for his first sessions of drama games he scheduled up to ten games for a 45-minute session. As he points out, "It's now obvious to me that no one could possibly get through the sheer volume of activity I had planned."

Anxiety to keep things going

Often there is a feeling that "I must keep the session moving at all times." First-time leaders frequently believe that if there is a lull in activity, participants will get bored — and they will have failed as a leader.

It is easy to place pressure on yourself. As you gain more experience and training, you will realize these lulls are valuable, offering time for participants to pause, reflect and discuss with each other how they feel.

Repetition is the key to success

There is often more to be learned about drama games and running drama workshops from the games that do not work than from those that do. If a game does not work 'well,' sit and think through the reasons why a particular game did not 'take off' with that particular group. The explanation may often be in simple things, such as:

- talking too much in your instructions when setting up the game;
- not demonstrating what you meant;
- not practising the game before you went in; and
- choosing an age-inappropriate game.

Often a game needs to be repeated in several sessions before some participants are able to internalize the rules. In some cases, participants do not really enjoy the game until they clearly understand the rules and have internalized them.

Cheating is a developmental milestone

This grows out of the last point. Once a group has internalized the rules of a game, almost inevitably one or more participants begin to 'cheat.' Often a leader's initial reaction is to intervene and inhibit the 'cheater' by telling them to stop. Actually the cheater has reached a milestone in understanding the rules, and is now able to play around with them.

However, if the cheater appears to be exploiting their peers, rather than saying 'Stop' change the rules; e.g., add an extra rule to make it harder for the cheater, or add a rule to bring everyone to the same level again.

Tim Dunne describes the result of over-strictness with rules: "In early sessions I tried to accomplish too much, taxing my clients' understanding of rule-bound games and making it difficult for them to become comfortable with drama games."

SUMMARY

To summarize the main points in planning and running the initial session:

1. The relationship between the leader and their group is crucial to the development of those engaged in drama games.
2. The leader must set the tone of the session, and create a safe environment in which the group members can be themselves without fear of danger or retribution from others.
3. Good preparation is the key to success.
4. Make sure you know what, if anything, is expected from you.
5. All one really needs for drama games to take place is a group and a space.
6. The ambience of the room is probably more important than its size.

13

7. Get to know your group.
8. Plan for your group's capabilities.
9. Establish ways to gain and hold your group's attention.
10. Aim for variety in the first session.
11. Introduce yourself.
12. Begin the first session with a name game. When meeting with a familiar group after a long break (e.g., summer or Christmas holidays), begin the first new session with a name game.
13. Explain each game clearly, slowly and, if necessary, with visual reinforcement. Model activities whenever possible.
14. Try to lead by example, making sure people know that you are prepared to participate and that you are not simply going to bark directions from the sidelines.
15. Try not to hurry the proceedings, and be patient with shy and reticent participants.
16. Allow participants to get to know the games and allow group members time to discuss and reflect on their experiences.
17. Do not be rigid about the rules of the game.
18. Do not be afraid to change the game.
19. Do not be too ambitious.
20. Try to relax and enjoy the proceedings. By doing this, you make it easier for he participants to enjoy themselves.
21. Be sensitive to the needs of the group.
22. Do not let the helpers overshadow the other players.
23. Always remain observant and open to suggestions.
24. Remember that your work is directed towards building confidence, trust and self-awareness in the hope that participants will find it easier to cope with social situations.

Remember, each new group will respond differently. Do not be surprised when a game that has worked well with every other group suddenly goes down like a 'lead balloon.' Do not worry about it — just begin another game. When the session is over, you can think about what might have caused this reaction.

It is important to remember that your sessions are only part of a person's life. It is essential that leaders cooperate with other professional staff (e.g., occupational therapists, psychologists and social workers). Attempt to make your sessions fit in with their views of the needs of the individuals in your group. This is particularly important when working in hospitals or other institutions. In addition, it is always helpful to be aware of daily routines.

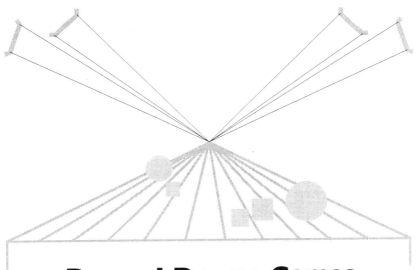

Beyond Drama Games

RUNNING REGULAR SESSIONS OF DRAMA GAMES

So far, I have concentrated on suggestions for running the first few games sessions. There are further things to consider when running sessions regularly.

1. Once your group has mastered the basic rules of the games, attempt to make the rules more complicated.
2. Try to reduce a player with a disability's need for a helper during the session. Encourage them to be more independent.
3. Encourage participants (particularly those with a disability) to have more and more say in running the sessions. Let them choose the games and encourage them to talk about those games they like and dislike.
4. Try experimenting with games — make up new games and new versions of old ones.

As well as these suggested aims, you might want to include music or relaxation activities in your games sessions. Another idea is to include games involving social situations, such as 'going shopping' or 'a train journey.' Do not be afraid to try out new ideas. Expect and accept that things will not always work and may even fail completely. In the long run, leadership is a mixture

15

of knowledge and experience. The latter cannot be taught — it has to be learned — and part of the process is learning from your mistakes.

MOVING INTO DRAMA AND THEATRE

There are many ways that your work in drama games can progress. I have already made some suggestions for developing your work beyond the first few sessions simply through a games-based approach. However, working with your group into longer, more developed, drama work (e.g., improvisational work, story drama) and into theatre, the performance aspect of drama can be very rewarding for you and the members of your group.

For leaders with limited experience or training in drama or theatre, the thought of developing work in these directions may at first be a little frightening. However, all of our lives are enmeshed in story and everyone has at least one story to tell. Consequently, story is often a very safe place to begin to develop your work from games into drama and theatre. In the practical activities section of this book you will find material on story-making and storytelling that was not included in earlier editions. These games and ideas can be used as springboards for the development of longer dramas, and even into performance for an invited audience. In addition to ideas in this book, there are several very good books to help you develop your ideas. As starting points, I recommend David Booth's *Story Drama* and Melanie Peter's *Drama For All*, as both have many ideas about how to organise and develop drama work.

For leaders interested in developing their work into theatre there are fewer reference materials available. However, as a starting point I suggest Richard Tomlinson's book *Disability, Theatre and Education* which although a little dated, may still be useful. Brian Way's book *Audience Participation: Theatre For Young People*, while not written specifically for work with people with a disability, also has many good ideas that you may find useful. In addition, I recommend watching the film *Feeling Good. Feeling Proud* (about the work of Theatre Unlimited), which is truly inspirational.

Finally, there is no imperative to develop your work in any particular direction. Each of us must find the path that takes us and our group on the journey that is appropriate to our skills and the group's needs. In your drama work, wherever it takes you, never forget to:

- start from where you and your group are;
- identify their needs and the context in which you work;
- work towards meeting their needs using the skills you have; and
- remember there is no one way of knowing, doing or being.

Working With Different Groups

INTRODUCTION

When I first started working with people with a disability, more often than not I worked with 'segregated' groups — individuals gathered together on the basis of a single defining label. During my first few years I ran drama games sessions for groups such as 'the mentally handicapped' and 'the blind.' The sessions I ran were valuable inasmuch as they did provide the people involved a chance to participate in drama activities, which some people involved was a first. These sessions allowed the participants an opportunity to develop as creative human beings, and for some it even provided an avenue of personal expression that eventually led to 'gainful' employment.

Segregated drama sessions, run specifically for a group whose primary connection was their 'disability,' always seemed to me to be going about things backwards. However, even today some of the reasons for working with a group whose members share similar challenges are still relatively sound. It is usually simpler to plan for a group with relatively similar challenges than for a group with a wide range of challenges. Nonetheless, in the initial stages of planning, new leaders working with such groups are more likely to consider the group's disability (the thing that defines it as a group) rather than

17

to look for the wide range of abilities that individuals in the group possess. Over the past twenty years, while the notions of segregation and separate-but-equal are still to be found, they have tended to be replaced by the concept of integration.

INTEGRATION AND DRAMA GAMES

Principles of integration are based on the strong philosophical belief that every person, regardless of their abilities or the challenges they face, has the right to as normal a lifestyle as possible. Currently, **deinstitutionalization** (the need to get people with severe disabilities out of institutions and back into their communities) and **mainstreaming** (the placement of people with severe disabilities in regular schools or age-appropriate classrooms, with special services as needed) are fast becoming the desired goals of most communities across North America.

However, integration is more of a philosophical commitment than a widely accepted practice. The process of integrating people with a disability back into our society is proving to be a difficult one. Despite social and legal directives to work towards full integration, decisions are still frequently made on the basis of a person's "disability" rather than their individuality.

THE PARADOX OF PLANNING

There is something strangely comical in considering an individual's needs on the basis of what they do not have. Yet all too often this is the way that drama activities are planned when working with a group that includes people with a disability. In preparing a drama session, leaders often spend too much time considering the challenges a person *faces* rather than considering what each individual is *able to do*.

The central paradox of planning is that all people are alike but different. While some of us face certain challenges created by physiological, anatomical or environmental factors, we all have our likes and dislikes, possess certain abilities, and face particular challenges in our daily lives. All human beings, irrespective of race, creed, colour or ability are fundamentally the same — but no two people, no matter how similar they may first appear, possess exactly the same capabilities.

When planning a drama session, attempting to solve this conundrum is not easy. There is no magic formula to apply, no single or simple solution. Each leader needs to create a process through which they can untie this knot to their own satisfaction.

In addition to the general points already mentioned, some other questions I consider when planning include:

- What do I need to know about each individual's capabilities and challenges? How do I ask the right questions?
- How can I make an activity accessible to the whole group?
- Can I find activities that help transform a perceived disability into a strength?

TOWARDS INTEGRATION

Implementing the basic principles of integration is not usually difficult in drama games sessions.

The global principles of integration (respect for the individual, knowledge that all persons have equal human rights, and an awareness that all people need support and care) are congruent with the basic principles of educational drama:

- there is no one way of being;
- start from where you are; and
- there is no single answer.

However, planning drama sessions that include players with a disability needs an **integrative** approach. An integrative approach emphasises an ongoing process whereby all players, irrespective of their capabilities, must work together in a mutually supportive fashion which acknowledges that all people are the same but different. In this process you should try to:

- enable all players to be active participants in the creative process;
- create an environment in which all participants, regardless of their abilities, are treated equally;
- recognize that each member of any group brings a variety of strengths and weakness, foibles and idiosyncrasies, to every session;
- plan activities that accentuate each player's strengths rather than identify their challenges;
- remember that in all groups the whole is stronger than the sum of the individual parts; and
- pair people together so that one person's strengths can help to compensate for another's area of challenge.

WORKING WITH PEOPLE WITH A PHYSICAL DISABILITY

Irrespective of the severity of the physical challenge, drama can have a valuable role to play in enriching a person's life and personal growth. In working with people with a physical disability,

19

there are a number of factors to consider over and above the general preparations outlined. You will always need to plan each drama session on the basis of the needs and abilities of the individuals in each particular group. The diversity and severity of physical challenges presented by each individual are essential pieces of information for planning the session. Often there is not enough time to plan for each individual's specific condition, but you must still be alert to the physical challenges faced by the individuals in your group. Initially, the root *cause* of a challenge (e.g., a restriction of locomotion) is not important; however, in the initial stages you have to provide experiences which meet the *physical needs* of each individual.

It is often helpful to ask yourself two questions:

1. How does the specific disabling condition affect the individuals' interactions with their environment? and
2. What stigmas are attached to their physical condition?

When running the session try to:

● Choose language appropriate to the age and life experiences of the group. At all costs avoid 'talking down' to the group.
● Get the group to work together. Teaming up an individual who uses a wheelchair and a person with a visual impairment can help to 'cancel out' their individual physical challenges.

This sharing of strengths and abilities is as important in groups who are brought together through a common denominator (e.g., spina bifida or epilepsy) as it is for a more 'mixed' group, since it enables the group to gain first-hand experience of working together to overcome specific physical challenges. It also enables them to see that everyone in the group is an individual and not just 'physically disabled.' This is an important change that must occur in both individual and social perceptions of disability if there is to be any chance of overcoming the stigmas which prevent people with a disability from participating fully in society.

WORKING WITH PEOPLE WITH A DEVELOPMENTAL DISABILITY

Under the guidance of a skilled leader, people with a developmental disability can be encouraged to make use of their imaginations, engage their emotions and as a result participate in drama and drama games.

People with a developmental disability, to greater or lesser degrees, suffer some form of delay which impedes the completion

20

of one or more tasks which we would normally take for granted. Different people find different tasks taxing, but the task in each case will present a greater problem in its successful completion than would be expected for an average individual at the same stage of development.

It is very important to be aware that not all tasks are affected uniformly. In fact many people with a developmental disability show 'islands of brilliance' where activities are undertaken and completed at a much higher level than might have been expected solely on observation and assessment of previous work. This is particularly true in creative areas such as drama and drama games.

No two people with a developmental disability are exactly alike. They come in all shapes and sizes, and there is no single 'prototype'; while certain specific conditions produce some similarity of physical characteristics, each individual is unique.

People with a developmental disability are not mentally ill; however, there may often be secondary emotional disorder which occurs as a result of social pressures, frustration, difficulties posed by communication and an inability to make themselves understood.

Contrary to popular opinion, people with a developmental disability are not always happy and obliging. As with everyone else, individuals experience a full range of emotions and moods.

The uniqueness of individuals with developmental delays makes planning very difficult.

There are, however, some basic ideas which may be helpful in preparing a drama games session for your group and all its hopes, fears, loves and hates.

Probably the most important facet of the session is the presentation of your material.

It is very important that you make yourself familiar with the language capabilities of your group, as communication of your material is essential to the success of a session.

When running a session try to:

- Choose your words carefully. Use language that is appropriate to the level of understanding of your group. However, don't simply reinforce the current language level but always attempt to stretch your group. This may be made easier for you if you are working with a mixed-ability group or with several helpers.
- Present and explain the games and activities in more than one way and always reinforce with gestural cues. In many cases it may be beneficial to model the activity (i.e., do a 'dry run' before asking your group to participate in the activity).

21

- Always allow ample *time* for the group members to familiarize themselves with *each* activity.
- Break the activities down into simple sections and progress step *by* step, always building on the previous stage.

Whenever appropriate, engage in conversation with your group before, during and after each activity or game. This communication provides you with essential feedback and allows the group to feel part of the decision-making process. An obvious exception is activities which require quiet and sensitivity, which do not lend themselves to discussion whilst in progress.

WORKING WITH SENIORS

Today, with the amazing advances of modern medicine, people are living longer. In addition, many people are able to live productive and vigorous lives well beyond the age of retirement. However, as we age, the body begins to greater or lesser degrees to show signs of 'wear and tear.' Injuries encountered in youth may 'play up' and degenerative conditions such as arthritis may play a part in affecting mobility and dexterity. Memory also may start to play tricks, with an increased potential for forgetfulness, loss of concentration or momentary loss of contact with the present. In addition, there is the spectre of debilitating and life-threatening conditions (e.g., Alzheimer's, cancer) which may create other challenges.

In working with seniors there are some additional factors that should be borne in mind:

- Seniors may be slow to become actively involved. Occasionally this may produce a 'wall of inertia' that has to be scaled prior to the start of each session.
- Some people will simply want to sit in their chair. (This should be interpreted literally!) Individuals often count a particular chair as their possession and woe betide the ignorant drama leader who sits in it by mistake.
- Many will see what you do as 'kids' stuff.' It is very difficult to introduce drama activities to seniors who have lived their lives by a 'Protestant work ethic.' They may think that play is for children and that games are played competitively or not at all.
- Some people will be over-anxious to participate. These over-willing volunteers need to be encouraged but not allowed to overshadow quieter members of the group or (more importantly) prevent the hesitant from joining in.

When running a session try to:

- Be prepared to work slowly. Activities will probably be interspersed with general discussion. In many cases the talking is as important, if not more important, than the activities.
- Develop a 'listener's ear' — it is important to be able to pick up on the concerns of the members of the group.
- Use language that is appropriate to the group; too often people talk to seniors as though they are children, which is terribly demeaning.
- Employ activities that emphasize the group's strengths (e.g., story-telling games, particularly those that allow individuals to dramatize personal tales).
- Choose games that will extend the group and get them moving. Start with chair-based movement games and then provide a reason for people to move out of their chairs. Too much of a senior's life is decided by other people without any reference to the individual's feelings. Activities that genuinely make them want to get up off their chair to dance or sing or act are essential to the development of the sessions.
- Select activities which allow for human contact in a non-threatening way. Many seniors in homes spend their lives isolated from human touch. The need to be hugged or touched can be very strong, but it can also be very frightening!

Also bear in mind that working in integrated and intergenerational groups can be a very valuable approach with seniors.

WORKING WITH INTERGENERATIONAL GROUPS

In addition to comments already made concerning integration, working with groups of different ages can be beneficial to all involved. This is particularly true when working with seniors.

Mixing generations can occur in many different ways. Some examples are by arranging for:

- your group to visit a 'retirement' home;
- a senior you know to visit your group (this works particularly well in elementary schools); and/or
- your group to include people of different ages.

All of us bring different temperaments, talents and experiences to a drama games session. Irrespective of age or ability we each have something to share with others.

Drama and drama games sessions provide each player an arena in which all participants are equals. The shared experience discov-

23

ered through playing creatively together can help to narrow the gap between generations.

In an intergenerational group the senior players often benefit from the energy and exuberance of the younger players, while the younger players often benefit from the wisdom and life experience of the seniors.

Seniors have a wealth of life experience that they can share with the group. Reminiscence techniques (such as storytelling using personal narratives) can be very valuable when working with seniors, particularly in intergenerational groups. Long-lived persons have often seen, heard and lived through experiences that younger people may not have had. They can provide a store of information about personal and social history that can be a valuable resource in a drama or drama games session.

Younger players can 'act out' the older players' stories, bringing old memories to life. Older players can control the narrative by using the word 'freeze' when they want to change an element. In this way they act as writer/director of their tale.

Through telling and dramatic re-playing, younger players can learn about how it was to live at a time before they were born, and can help keep senior players' memories alive.

Practical
Activities

INTRODUCTION

When working with the games in the next section, keep the following in mind:

- There are no right or wrong answers.
- Initially, being accepted by the group and enjoying the activities is the only 'success' needed by players.
- When playing touch games, some players enjoy being touched and others do not.
- Some players become scared when asked to wear a blindfold. Ask these players to simply close their eyes and keep them closed. They may occasionally cheat. If this happens, you can change the rules, usually by adding an extra rule to make it harder for the cheater.
- To have successful drama games sessions, you must plan for *your* group's capabilities, likes and dislikes.

Each game should include three phases: *rehearsal*, *repetition* and *review*.

Rehearsal
Allow yourself time to:

1. explain the activity clearly; and
2. demonstrate the activity for the group.

Also, allow time for players to practise the activity — take a 'trial' run.

Repetition

Allow yourself time to:

1. observe players' interpretations of the activity; and
2. provide assistance to players when necessary.

Allow time for players to attempt the activity several times, affording them the opportunity to make mistakes.

Review

After players have mastered the simple rules of the activity, allow yourself time to:

1. supply more complicated rule(s); and
2. share players' variations with the group.

Allow time for players to:

1. discuss the game, if desired; and
2. attempt the variations suggested by you and other players.

Some games allow players to spend a great deal of time repeating and reviewing their experiences.

All the games on the following pages can be adapted for use with a wide range of players. Feel free to do so. However, be aware that some games are more easily adapted for specific group needs than others.

ADAPTING FOR INTEGRATION

- Do not make assumptions about the capabilities of players in your group based solely on labels. For example, do not exclude players who use a wheelchair from a game that requires the group to stand in a circle. Any game that requires standing can be adapted for players who use a wheelchair or who have difficulty standing.
- Do not simply allow someone to say, 'I can't do that because....' With relatively few exceptions it has been my experience that 'where there is a will there is a way.'
- Whenever and wherever possible, talk to each player with a disability about how you can help them participate in a game.
- Work together with the players in your group to try to find solutions to obstacles.
- Through discussion and trial and error, most games can be adapted so that all players in the group can participate. Some-

times the structure and/or rules of the game are changed, but the essence of the activity remains. Through this process many new games are discovered.

USEFUL EQUIPMENT

It is possible to make use of almost anything in a drama games session. Objects can be used imaginatively — a chair can become a throne or can simply be a chair. With a little imagination, the furniture and the room become part of your equipment.

However, there are a few things, essential to some games, which are not usually found in every room. I suggest that for every session you bring the following items with you, or arrange for them to be available to you:

- balloons;
- hats;
- odd bits of material or scarves for blindfolds;
- a cup (for **Computer**);
- string and scissors;
- objects suitable for passing around a circle;
- a tape recorder or record player;
- a few rostra blocks to allow different levels;
- a dressing box — masks and make-up;
- paints, pencils, crayons, and paper; and
- simple musical instruments, especially percussive ones.

At-A-Glance
Guide to Games

SKILL AREAS ASSOCIATED WITH GAMES

The letters preceding each skill area below are used in the game index (on the next page), to assist you in selecting the most appropriate games for your players.

A. Social integration

Social Integration games are helpful in the following areas:

- acquiring skills necessary to good social functioning;
- building cooperation and trust with peers; and
- understanding the rules of social performance or generally improving social interactions.

B. Creativity and self-expression

Creativity and Self-Expression games are helpful in the following areas:

- developing expressive and receptive language;
- encouraging sensory awareness; and
- enhancing imagination, spontaneity and abstract thought.

C. Body awareness and physical control

Body Awareness and Physical Control games are helpful in the following areas:

- acquiring physical dexterity and control;
- developing awareness of body schema and body image;
- providing outlets for emotional and physical energies; and
- practising impulse control.

D. Cognitive skill development

Cognitive Skill Development games are helpful in the following areas:

- enhancing memory and recall;
- developing concentration;
- encouraging reflectivity;
- practising anticipation of consequences; and
- comprehending and solving problems.

E. Observation

Observation games may provide leaders with insight in the following areas:

- styles of improvisation;
- social competence; and
- temperament and sense of humour.

GAMES INDEX

The Games Index provides easy reference to all the games that follow. Each game listing has the game title, associated skill area letter codes (described above), and the page number the game appears on. Games shown with a star (*) beside their name may also be used as a warm-up game.

Game Type/Name	Skill Area	Page
NAME GAMES 33		
Name Game*	A,C	33
Name Game (Catch)*	A,B,D	33
Introductions*	A,B	34
Strangers*	A,B,E	34
Sounds Like My Name*	A,B	34
Shapes of My Name*	A,B,C	35
Echo*	A	35

NAME GAMES

Names are very important. For some players their name may be the most significant thing in that individual's life and the only thing to which they respond consistently.

It is *very* important to play name games in the first few sessions so that people can get to know one another. It is also valuable to play a name game after a holiday or even a week or two's break between sessions.

❏ Name Game

There are many variations of this game and most are played sitting in a circle. This is no exception.

How to Play: The simplest version is for the leader to ask each player to say their own name as the leader points to them.

The leader should go around the circle two or three times, repeating each name after it has been said. Some players may need extra help saying their names.

❏ Name Game (Catch)

This is a variation of **Name Game** above.

How to Play: Once the players have introduced themselves, hand a soft 'nerf' ball to one of them.

Ask that player to throw (or give) it to another player. The catcher has to say the thrower's name. If the player gets it wrong or can't remember it, the ball is handed back to the thrower, who repeats their own name and then throws the ball to a new catcher. When the catcher gets the thrower's name right, they become the new thrower.

33

Materials required: A soft nerf ball (or any soft foam ball) about the size of a soccer ball.

This game can be complicated and may need to be simplified for your group. Often the catcher will say their own name or other players will say the thrower's name. Also, not all the players may be able to catch, so the thrower may have to become a giver.

❏ **Introductions**

How to Play: Pair off players one with another, and allow time for all players to get to know one another.

Then ask them to introduce each other to the rest of the group.

Notes:
1. If your group has one or more players with communication or speech difficulties, assign helpers to partner these players.
2. The sensitivity and the degree of verbal skill possessed by the players will determine the amount of information exchanged.
3. During the introductions some players may need help from their partners.

❏ **Strangers**

How to Play: Ask players to move freely around the room. Tell them that they should introduce themselves to one another. Ask them to try to find out as much information as they can about each of the people they meet.

After a short while ask the group to come back into a circle to share what they found out from meeting one another.

Variation(s):   A variation is for the leader to control the game using a signal, e.g., "change," to tell the players to move to another person. The length of time can then be varied, e.g., shortening the time allowed to speak each time "change" is called. The final call can be "You have 30 seconds to meet everybody you haven't spoken to."

Afterwards discuss how the players felt about the time allowed to greet and meet others.

❏ **Sounds Like My Name**
The group is seated in a circle for this game.

How to Play: One at a time each player says or sings their name anyway they want.

Variation(s): Saying names softly, normally or loudly; clapping the rhythm of the name as a group; and chanting the name as a group.

Other variations are **Shapes of My Name** and **Echo**, below.

❑ Shapes of My Name

The group is seated in a circle for this game.

How to Play: One at a time each player says their name and, at the same time, creates a shape either with a gesture or with the whole body.

❑ Echo

The group is seated in a circle for this game.

How to Play: One at a time, each player says their name any way they like and the rest of the group responds by echoing the sound and/or shape.

WARM-UP GAMES

Every session that you lead is different. It is important that the games you choose to start your sessions will warm up players for the type of games you intend to play that day.

If you are going to do a lot of storytelling work perhaps a **vocal warm-up game** will be helpful. However, if you intend to work with a lot of high-energy games you will better serve your group by choosing a **physical warm-up game**.

Physical/Non-Verbal Games

These games are useful in preparing the body for action. They can be considered all-purpose warm-ups for Physical and High-Energy games. Some games help prepare the group for Body Awareness games and for Collaborative games.

❑ Rob's Little Finger Game

This game requires a lot of space for players to move around.

How to Play: Ask the players to find themselves some space (assist players in doing so, as necessary).

Then ask players to raise their right arm and wiggle the thumb of their right hand.

Then ask them to wiggle the fingers on their left hand while keeping their right thumb moving. Gradually increase the number of parts of the body players are moving until

35

they are moving both arms, both legs, wrists, knees, fingers and elbows, and are hopping around the room humming "God Save the Queen" (or another well-known tune).

This is a difficult game but an enjoyable one. Amend it as the physical capabilities of the group demand.

❑ Body Writing

The group spreads about the room so that each person has their own space.

How to Play: Ask the group to imagine that they are standing in front of a chalkboard. Then tell them to imagine they are attaching a piece of chalk to a specified part of the body (e.g., the elbow). Then ask the group to write on the board using the piece of chalk.

Variation(s): People can work in pairs, taking turns to be a human blackboard.
Use different parts of the body to write with.

Keep instructions simple and specific (e.g., write the letter A or the number 6). This can progress to writing names or sentences in joined-up writing.

❑ People to People

This game requires an odd number of players.

How to Play: Divide the group into pairs. The remaining player is IT.
IT calls anatomical commands such as "hand to hand". Pairs respond by placing the identified body parts together.
At any time, the player who is IT may call "People to People," at which point players must find new partners. The player left without a partner becomes IT.

Variation(s): As a variation, at the "People to People" command, have players thank their partners before searching for new partners. As the game progresses, it may be appropriate to make the instructions more difficult, e.g., "right thumb to left knee."

❑ Tag

This is a simple version of tag.

How to Play: One player is IT. The other players run away.

IT tries to tag one of the other players. When a player is tagged, that player becomes the new IT.

Variation(s): There are a 1,001 variations on tag, e.g.:
- Each new IT decides how the group (including IT) must move.
- Each tagged player joins IT's team so that the number of players who are IT increases, until all but one player is IT. That one player then becomes the first IT in the next game.

❏ Chickens

If the group is too light-headed after this game, follow it with a short relaxation session.

How to Play: Instruct players to blow their noses. Then tell them to breathe only through their noses, and to use their arms like chicken's wings.

While breathing, they should expel the air out of their lungs. Have the players continue this method of expelling air from their lungs for up to a couple of minutes, nonstop. Remind players to keep their mouths closed during the exercise.

Variation(s):
- Moving around the room while "chicken breathing."
- Playing with breathing rhythms and turning the movement into dance with its own musical (breathing) accompaniment.

Materials required: A box of paper tissues.

This game can also be combined with **Hunters** (see below) to create **Chicken and Hunter Tag** (see p. 53).

❏ Hunters

This game may need to be adapted for particular groups but is a fun way of breathing fully. If the group is too excited after this game, follow it with a short relaxation session.

How to Play: Ask the players to imagine they have an axe in either hand.

Ask them to cleave the air with the axe. Tell the players to keep repeating the sound "who" while hopping from one leg to the other and cleaving the air with their axes.

Variation(s):   Variations of this game include modifying the rhythms and turning the movement and sound into dance.

❑ Four Walls, a Floor and a Ceiling

How to Play: Give your group a certain time (e.g., one minute) in which *everyone* must touch the four walls of the room, the floor and the ceiling. Watch how much or how little they cooperate.

Variation(s):   Add windows, doors, items of specific colours or textures to the list.

Get the group to touch things using their feet, noses or heads.

❑ Chair Swap

How to Play: Place chairs in a circle facing inwards. Each player sits in a chair, except one player who stands in the centre of the circle. This player is IT.

The seated players look around the circle trying to make eye contact with someone else. As soon as they make contact they must change places. As they do so, IT tries to sit in one of the empty chairs. Whoever is left without a chair is the new IT.

Variation(s):   IT can determine who changes places by calling out who may change, e.g.: anyone with fair hair; anyone wearing something blue; anyone who hates school dinners; anyone who had muesli for breakfast; etc.

IT can also determine the way people move across the circle: hopping, baby steps, shake hands in the middle, etc.

In another variation an extra chair is added to the circle. However, just before IT sits down the person sitting next to the empty chair moves to their right and sits in it. Immediately the next person in the circle moves to their right...and so on around the circle. This makes it very hard indeed for IT to sit in an empty chair and not on somebody's lap.

Materials required: One chair for every player except the person who is IT.

❑ Follow My Dance

The group sits in a well-spaced circle so that each player can see every other player.

How to Play: The leader then puts on some music and starts to move to it. The group tries to copy the leader's movements. After a while the leader then says "Let's all follow [**player's name**]."

The player named then becomes the dance leader. After a while the leader instructs the group to follow another player's lead. And so the game continues, with different players taking the lead.

As the group becomes familiar with each other and with this game, each player can choose the next leader of the dance.

Materials required: Music, a tape/CD/record player, and some chairs.

It may be helpful to require that all players stay in contact with their chairs, particularly where working with large groups or groups with mixed physical abilities.

Suitable music is a matter of taste. Simon and Garfunkel's "Greatest Hits," Fleetwood Mac's "Rumours," and Phil Collins' "Face Value" work well. Baroque music, e.g., Pachelbel's "Canon," and almost any song by the Beatles have also proved successful.

Vocal Games

These games are important in preparing players for storytelling work as they help prevent players from overworking or straining their voice.

❏ Heart of a Breath

Heart of a Breath is excellent preparation for vocal or physical work, and is also a very good way of calming a group down.

How to Play: Once the group is standing in a circle, ask them to:
- stand feet parallel to one another about shoulder width apart;
- keep knees slightly bent, so that weight is evenly distributed between both feet;
- tuck hips slightly forward so that their back is naturally straight and the shoulders are slightly rounded;
- place hands palm down with thumbs on navel, fingertips on the pubic bone so as to form a heart shape between their hands;
- close eyes and mouth and breathe in and out through their nose;

39

- 'guide' their breath into the heart shape over the lower abdomen;
- breathe slowly and smoothly, with as little effort as possible; and
- try to keep breathing as regularly as possible.

Heart of a Breath is easily adapted for players who use wheelchairs or who have difficulty standing, by simply allowing them to sit as part of the circle.

❏ Wall of Names

The group stands in a circle.

How to Play: Ask players to:
- imagine that arms are birds' wings; and
- synchronize breathing with arm movements so that in-breath is coordinated with upward movement of arms, and out-breath with downward motion.

Once the group's arm movements are synchronized:
- add sound to the movement using the names of the people in your group;
- ask each person to say their name on the out-breath in the style of a Gregorian chant, e.g., "Ber......nie.......";
- on the next out-breath ask the group to repeat the chant of that person's name; and
- continue around the group until everyone has said their name and has had the group echo it.

This is a good game to follow **Heart of a Breath** (above).

❏ Sounds Across the Circle

How to Play: Once the group is standing in a large circle (facing inwards), ask them to imagine that their names can be formed into a 'ball of sound.'

Putting as much of their body into the throw as possible, one player 'throws' their 'name ball' across the circle to someone who catches it.

The catcher then throws their own name to someone else. This continues until all members of the group have thrown their name across the circle.

Variation(s):   Once the group has the idea of throwing names across the circle, there are several variations that can be tried.
- Use vowel sounds instead of names, i.e., "ah," "oo," "ee," etc.

40

- Use natural sounds, e.g., wind, sea, animals.
- Use any sound, e.g., "boing-boing."

Once the group has mastered throwing sounds across the circle:

- ask each player to move across the circle as they say their sound;
- ask the rest of the group to echo the sound as the player moves across the circle;
- ask player to move in a way suggested by the sound they are making; and
- ask the circle to make the sound and ask one player to move across the circle in a way suggested by the group's sound.

This game works well after **Wall of Names** (above) or **Echo** (see p. 35).

❏ Talk, Whisper, Shout

Divide the players into groups of three.

How to Play: Direct the players in each group to converse on any given topic.

Of the three, one player speaks in a normal tone of voice, another shouts, and the remaining player whispers.

At various times during the conversation, call "freeze." The players then stop conversing and the leader changes the 'volume' of each speaker (e.g., the whisperer becomes the shouter, the shouter becomes the talker, and the talker becomes the whisperer).

To avoid players straining their voices it is advisable to play **Wall of Names** (see p. 40) before this game.

❏ Bing Bong

The group stands or sits in a circle.

How to Play: The leader explains that players turn their heads to the right when they say "Bing" and to the left when they say "Bong." Practice by passing the word "Bing" around the circle and then the word "Bong" around the circle. When the group has a sense of the game, add variations.

Variation(s):
- passing the words around the circle as quickly as possible;
- changing the direction associated with the words;

41

- throwing the words across the circle by making eye contact with another player; and
- changing words from "Bing" and "Bong" to other words or sounds.

Creative/Group Games

These games are useful in preparing players for improvisational and storytelling games. Some games also help prepare the group for collaborative work and may be helpful in preparing for Trust and Sensitivity Games (see p. 58).

❑ Will You Change Places With Me?

This game starts with the group sitting in a circle.

How to Play: The leader then asks one player if they would like to change places. The two leave the safety of their chairs, exchange greetings and positive comments with each other (e.g., "My name is John. I really like your new shoes") and then swap positions in the circle. The player now in the leader's place asks another player to swap places.

This game continues until all players have had the opportunity to initiate the exchange.

❑ Male or Female?

This game should be played before other touch games, to determine how individual players respond to being touched.

How to Play: A player sits on a chair in the centre of a circle with their eyes shut.

One at a time, other players gently touch the player in the centre. The seated player has to guess whether the person touching them is male or female. The game continues until all players who want a turn in the centre have had one.

Sometimes this game is turned into a competition by some players, who are bitterly disappointed if they guess incorrectly.

❑ Whose Hands Are These?

This game is a variation of **Male or Female**, above.

How to Play: A player (Player #1) sits in the centre of the circle with their eyes closed and their hands resting on their knees palm up.

One at a time other players approach the person in the middle and place their hands palm down on top of Player #1's hands.

Player #1 tries to determine who is in front of them through an examination of the person's hands.

☐ Do As I Do

This is a very simple follow-the-leader game in which the group has to do exactly what the leader does.

How to Play: The leader can perform an action or describe the action (e.g., "touch your nose").

As long as the actions are simple, there should be very few problems with this game.

This game can be followed by similar games like **Simon Says** (not included in this list) where players have to distinguish between two kinds of commands — one which they must follow and the other which they must ignore.

☐ What Am I Feeling?

This is an introductory mime game for a group which may be unfamiliar with mime.

How to Play: The leader should mime feeling angry, happy, sad, depressed, excited, etc.

The group has to guess what emotion the leader is feeling.

Variation(s): Two variations of this game are **What's My Job?** and **What Am I Doing?** (both not included in this list). Again, these are both very introductory mime exercises. In each, the leader mimes a sequence of actions and the players have to guess what the leader is doing or what job they are performing. For example, if the leader is miming a mail carrier, the leader will walk along and post letters, etc.

Other variations include:
- allow players one at a time to lead the activity;
- ask the group to work in pairs; and
- have one player mime while the other guesses the job.

☐ Liar's Tag

This game is played with the group in a circle.

How to Play: The leader mimes an activity (e.g., brushing their teeth).

The player to the leader's right (Player #1) then asks the leader what they are doing. The leader continues to mime the activity but lies about what they are doing (e.g.,

"Oh, I am playing tennis"). The leader then stops their action.

Player #1 then starts to mime whatever the leader says they were doing (e.g., playing tennis). This sequence continues around the circle, with each player lying about their action to the player questioning them and then the questioning player performing the 'lied about' action.

❑ Instant Response (Look, Hold, Become)

This game has three distinct stages and three sets of commands.

How to Play: The group begins by spreading out around the room. In the first stage, the leader asks the players to look at things: "Look at the ceiling," "Look at the floor," etc.

Humorous requests like "Look at the back of your own head" are very popular as long as it is clear they are meant to be funny.

In the next stage, the players pretend to hold objects. Sample commands include: "Imagine you are holding a furry cat in your hands"; "Imagine you are holding an ice cream"; or "Imagine you are holding a bowl brim-full of water." **You may need to reinforce commands by acting out the necessary action.**

The third stage of the game is to *become* something. Start the players off with inanimate objects with commands like "Become a telegraph pole" or "Become the number 7," and then move on to commands like "Become a police officer."

It is possible to move from stage three into more structured drama.

❑ Dracula

This is a good game to use after any of the name games (see p. 33), and is an enjoyable way to learn players' names.

How to Play: The group sits or stands in a circle with the leader in the centre. The leader is Dracula.

The players are told that Dracula can sit down only after 'killing' someone. Dracula does this by touching their victim on the back of the neck with their index finger. The 'dead' victim then exchanges places with Dracula, becoming the new Dracula.

To avoid being killed, the intended victim stares at someone in the circle. The player receiving the stare has

44

to say the victim's name before Dracula strikes. Thus thwarted, Dracula must look for a new victim.

Materials required: A useful item would be a cloak or cape.

Sometimes the entire group will come to the rescue of the victim or sometimes the victim will say their own name. Be prepared to modify the rules.

COLLABORATIVE GAMES

Most drama games demand a degree of collaboration if they are to be successful. However, the following games require the group to work together, either to solve a problem or to confuse or 'outfox' one or more players who are IT.

❑ **Yes Let's**

How to Play: Any member of the group makes a suggestion, e.g., "Let's all stand by the window."

The rest of the group summon up all their enthusiasm and shout, "Yes, let's!" and then move over to the window. Someone else suggests, "Let's all whistle the National Anthem." The rest shout, "Yes, let's!" and do so. The game continues to a natural conclusion.

Variation(s): As a variation you can introduce "No, let's...," where someone makes an alternative suggestion to each call; e.g., "Let's all count to ten." "No, let's all stand on one leg." The group divides into two teams according to which of the suggestions they prefer, then the game begins again.

❑ **Scales**

How to Play: Explain that the length of the room represents a scale upon which people are going to place themselves according to their own perceptions of themselves.

Ask the group to stand in order of height, with the tallest person at one end of the scale and the shortest at the other. This is a nice clear example in which the rules of the game can be illustrated.

Then ask players to place themselves on a scale in order of their age. Obviously some people will have to move.

The next scale could be decided by eye colour: dark at one end and very light at the other.

45

If it is appropriate, the group can now move on to look at more complicated scales:

- the degree of their individual ambition;
- level of personal happiness;
- left-/right-wing politics;
- self-confidence; etc.

The group will often have suggestions to make, and you can use this exercise to look more closely at issues raised elsewhere in the session.

Some of the decisions will be harder to make than others.

Always allow players to 'opt out' of making a statement without fear of stigmatization.

❑ Fruit Bowl

The group sits in a circle with a player in the middle who is IT.

How to Play: Everyone in the outer circle says the name of a fruit out loud for the others to hear. The names must all be different.

IT tries to say the name of somebody's chosen fruit three times, very quickly (e.g., "Banana, Banana, Banana"). The player who chose this fruit must say Banana (only once) before IT has finished saying it three times. If the player succeeds, IT turns to somebody else and tries to beat them (e.g., by saying "Apple, Apple, Apple"). If IT does say "Apple" three times before the appropriate player can say it once, they change places and the retiring IT becomes the apple. The new IT takes over until they beat someone and inherit the name of their fruit. After a few goes the game becomes very fast and very confusing.

Variation(s): Use other sets of objects (animals, flowers, famous people).

Use people's own names to reinforce an introductory name game (but do not change names each time IT retires or you'll end up even more confused!).

❑ Master and Slave

This game was originally a Victorian parlour game. The title is itself an anachronism which leaders may wish to change. This game needs an odd number of players.

How to Play: Divide the group into pairs, leaving one player without a partner.

The pairs face the same direction, one in front of the other, so that the group forms two circles facing the centre.

46

One member of each pair is in the inner *seated* circle (slaves) and the other is in the outer *standing* circle (masters).

The player without a partner stands in the outer circle behind a vacant chair, which is part of the inner circle. This player must try to 'win' another master's 'slave' by winking at the 'slave.'

Once winked at, the slave tries to escape to the vacant chair while their current master attempts to prevent escape by gently tapping the slave on the shoulder.

Materials required: Enough chairs to seat *half* the group.

This game requires careful thought as to who should be a master and who a slave. The important considerations are the degree of physical mobility and whether players can wink.

This game can get very physical, so extra rules may be necessary to restrain over-possessive masters. It is up to the leader's discretion to decide when a slave has 'escaped,' e.g., immediately after leaving a chair, only when safely in the other chair, etc.

❑ Court of the Holy Dido

This is a 'ritualistic' game that was used by actors to help prepare for performances of comic plays. Once learned, this is one of the most popular group games. Adolescents particularly seem to want to play it again and again.

How to Play: The group sits on chairs in a circle so that everyone can see everybody else. A large balloon (The Holy Dido) is at the leader's feet.

The leader informs the group that they are *The Court of the Holy Dido.* All players are referred to by number only, except the leader who is known as "O Worshipful Master." Assign each player a number. Tell the group that from the moment the court is in session they may not speak each other's names but must refer to one another by their assigned number.

Remind players that the court meets rarely and it sits only to observe its own rules, which all members have sworn to uphold. Tell the players that soon the court will be convened, but first you will remind them of the rules.

The rules of the court are:
- you must sit right arm crossed over left;
- you must sit right leg crossed over left; and
- you must remain silent and you must not smile.

47

It is the solemn duty of each member of the court to inform the Master of the court of any person who breaks the rules. To do this they must:

- stand;
- ask for permission to speak;
- upon gaining permission to speak from the Master, describe who has broken what rule;
- the Master will then deliberate and announces the punishment — usually several blows from the Holy Dido to be inflicted on the rule-breaker by the informer;
- upon administering punishment the member of the court places the Holy Dido at the Master's feet;
- kneeling, they say, "I return the Holy Dido O Worshipful Master; permission to sit down";
- only after gaining permission may they sit down.

Once all the rules and procedures have been covered say, "The court is now in session."

Variation(s):   The Master changes the rules of the court in mid-session.

The Master passes the leadership of the court to a court member. The Master now takes that player's number.

If, as leader, you allow another to be master, it is *very* important that you retain power to bring the court to a close. Finding a creative way to do this may be challenging.

❑ Computer

This game is best begun as a demonstration with a helper playing the 'computer.'

How to Play: A helper sits on a chair in the centre of the circle of players with a cup of water in front of them.

Another player comes and sits on a chair facing the helper.

The helper is the computer and the other player is the programmer. The programmer uses simple commands (extend right arm, stop, lower, stop, etc.) to program the computer to drink from the cup. The computer can only do what the helper 'programs' them to do.

The two most important commands are "stop," which should follow every command, and "swallow," which must be given as the computer is about to drink.

Materials required: Chairs and a cup of water.

48

This is a great game and can be extended to include all the players as assistants to the programmer. Be warned that the computer is likely to get very wet.

❑ **Hand Squeeze**

How to Play: In this game, the players stand in a circle and join hands. The leader attempts to pass a message around the circle.

To pass the message "number three," the leader squeezes their neighbour's hand three times. The message is passed from hand to hand around the circle.

After successfully passing a message around the circle in one direction, try to pass one in the other direction.

Variation(s):   After this, try two directions at once. This might meet with failure but is very enjoyable.

Another variation is to place a player in the centre of the circle and ask them to determine where the message is. They can do this by pointing to the player they think has just received the message or by calling out the suspect's name. When the player in the centre has correctly identified the position of the message, they change places with the player who has been caught.

The leader must keep a close watch on the proceedings to ensure fair play.

❑ **Ring on a String**

The group sits in a circle with one player in the centre.

How to Play: The string is threaded through the ring. It is then passed around the circle so that the players can hold it with both hands and so keep the string taut. The string is then tied tightly.

The idea is to pass the ring around the circle (on the string) without the player in the centre knowing where it is.

Before each round of the game, the player in the centre has to close their eyes for a few seconds so that the ring can be passed around the circle.

The player in the centre must find the ring by tapping another player's hands. When a hand is tapped it must be opened immediately. If the ring is underneath it, the player in the centre changes places with the player hiding the ring. If not, the game continues.

Materials required: Ball of string, a ring.

For the game to work well, the string must be taut and the players must open their hands as soon as they are touched. Also the string must be strong.

Be warned, rings have been known to disappear.

❑ **Passing the Object Around the Circle**

The game is similar to **Ring on a String**, above.

How to Play: This time, objects (balloons, tennis balls, lamp stands) are passed around behind the backs of the players in the circle while the player in the centre has to guess where the object is.

As in **Ring on a String**, the player in the centre will have to close their eyes for a few seconds before the start of each game.

The centre player touches players one at a time, who then have to bring their arms from behind their backs. If the 'tagged' player is holding an object, they change places with the player in the centre. If the 'tagged' player is not holding an object the game continues with the same player in the centre.

Variation(s): This game can be made more complicated by passing more than one object around the circle at any one time. This will probably cause confusion, not least to the player in the centre.

Materials required: Objects to pass around the circle (e.g., hats, balloons, etc.).

❑ **Chinese Whispers (Telephone)**

How to Play: Players sit in a circle. The leader whispers a short phrase in the ear of the player sitting on their right.

This player then whispers that phrase to the person on their right and so on until the phrase reaches the player on the leader's left. At this point, the initial and final phrases are compared. It is usually funny to see how the phrase changed as it went around the circle.

❑ **Backboard**

This game is a variation on **Chinese Whispers**, above.

How to Play: Players sit on the floor in a circle, facing the next player's back.

The object of the game is to pass a word around the circle by writing on the back of the player in front of them.

50

The leader starts by writing on the back of the player in front of them. The leader uses only capital letters to form the word and passes one word at a time. When the word has gone around the circle, players compare the initial word with the final word.

Variation(s): Variations include passing single letters, shapes or even short phrases.

Keep the words short and simple. Remember, the bigger the circle, the more difficult it is to pass the word around.

❏ Killer

This is a well-known party game.

How to Play: Players stand in a circle in such a way that they are able to see the other players. Once in position the players close their eyes.

While the players' eyes are closed, the leader walks around the group and touches one of them. This player is the killer.

The leader now tells the group to open their eyes. Each player then looks around the circle and holds another's gaze. The killer kills by winking at their victim, who silently counts to three then drops dead.

Players put their hands up when they think they know who the killer is. When two players have their hands up, the leader asks them to point at the player they think is the killer. If they both point to the same player and they are right, that is the end of the game. If they are wrong, or point to different players, the game continues until either the killer is discovered or all the players are killed.

Variation(s): For variety, you may want to play **Danish Murder** (see below).

In this game, players are supposed to fix each others gaze for a few seconds — however, some players simply pan around the circle or are unable to wink. If a player cannot wink, suggest they blink instead.

❏ Danish Murder

How to Play: The group spreads about the room. All the players, except the leader, close their eyes.

The leader chooses a murderer by touching the player on the shoulder (initially it may help if the player is a helper).

51

The group is then told to walk around the room with their eyes closed and their hands out in front of them. When they meet someone, they greet them by tapping three times on the stranger's hands. If the stranger replies to the tap, they are both safe. If no tap comes in reply, they have been murdered.

Variation(s): Another variation is to allow the murderer to keep their eyes open.

As with **Killer**, above, there are some problems associated with this game. Some killers do the opposite of what they are supposed to do. There is also the problem of players not keeping their eyes closed. I recommend playing this game with the added attraction of a prize for the best death to help alleviate this problem.

❑ Belly Laugh

This game is best played on a clean carpet or floor.

How to Play: The first player lies down on their back on the floor.

The next player lies down on their back with their head on the stomach of the first player. Each new player lies down with their head on the stomach of the player before until all players are lying down on their backs.

Every player, except the first and last, will have their head on another player's stomach and another player's head on their stomach. Player #1 then says "Ha," Player #2 says "Ha, ha," Player #3 says "Ha, ha, ha," and so on down the line. When the game works, all the players are laughing uproariously before the end.

Variation(s): A variation of this game is to have players tell jokes while they are lying on the floor. The rule then is that the joke must not make anyone laugh.

PHYSICAL/HIGH-ENERGY GAMES

The games in this section *may* pose problems for less mobile players. However, most of the games can be adapted to meet the needs of players who face mobility challenges; e.g., when working with integrated or intergenerational groups you may wish to add extra rules to 'handicap' more mobile players.

It is also particularly advisable throughout these games to keep an 'extra eye' out for people with mobility challenges. If a player has severe medical problems it may be helpful to have a helper **shadow** them. Shadowing has been used as a technique for several years by summer camps which integrate persons with profound disabilities. A player with profound medical or physical challenges may be assigned a 'shadow' — a helper — whose job is to follow the player throughout the games. The shadow allows the player complete independence and will intervene only if they put themselves in a position of danger. The shadow should attempt to interact as little as possible with the player, so as to avoid establishing a dependent relationship.

❏ Tick

Split the group into pairs; one player of each pair is designated Left and the other Right.

How to Play: The player who is Right tries to touch their partner's right hand using their own right hand.

Left tries to touch their partner's left hand using their own left hand. After a while players are asked to change roles.

If this proves a bit complicated, try a simpler version. Each player attempts to touch their partner in the small of the back while their partner tries to avoid being 'ticked.'

❏ Magnets

The group divides into pairs.

How to Play: Partners run about the room separate from one another. When they catch sight of their partner they run towards each other only to be instantly repelled. They are like poles of a conventional magnet and no matter how hard they try they cannot touch each other.

Variation(s): Partners become weak electro-magnets: no sooner do they make contact than the current is reversed and they are once again repelled.

❏ Chicken and Hunter Tag

Having played both **Chickens** (p. 37) and **Hunters** (p. 37), divide the group into chickens and hunters.

How to Play: Hunters then chase the chickens. When tagged, chickens become hunters.

Variation(s): Variations include beginning with only one hunter and having chickens drop out of the game after they have been tagged.

Have players silently choose to become either a chicken or a hunter.

53

❑ The Farmer's Animals

Divide the group into three smaller groups. Each group plays a different 'herd' (cows, sheep, pigs, etc.), and each must choose one group member to be the farmer.

How to Play: This being done, the farmer and their herd go to opposite ends of the room.

The animals then close their eyes. The farmer calls the herd by making the appropriate animal sound. The leader then allows one of each herd out at a time. The farmer who collects the entire head first is the winner.

Variation(s): As a variation, the group can be split up into four or five smaller groups. Each group is a different animal (cow, cat, pig, dog, etc.). The players then close their eyes and move around the room. At a given signal, with their eyes still closed and using only their animal's sound, they all try to find the other members of their animal group. This can be a very noisy game with all the animals trying to find each other.

Before you let the animals loose, make sure the players know what sound their animal makes.

❑ Bombs Away

Label the four walls of the room front, back, right and left.

How to Play: Having explained the four directions, instruct the players to move to the side of the room called out and then proceed to call out one direction at a time.

Begin with a couple of practice runs to acquaint the players with the different directions. Then mix up the instructions — front, right, left, back, etc. At a point during the game, call "Bombs Away!" At the "Bombs Away" command, players should lie down on the ground.

Note: Take care that players do not drop too quickly to the ground, banging their heads or otherwise injuring themselves.

This is a very good game to practice directionality. Nautical terms (port, starboard), colours, letters or numbers can be substituted for the directions.

❑ Breaking Out

The group, with the exception of two players, forms a very tight circle by linking arms.

How to Play: One of the two remaining players stays inside the circle while the other goes outside the circle.

The player outside now attempts to get inside and the one on the inside tries to get outside, while the players forming the circle attempt to stop both of them.

This can be a very physical game.

❑ Mountain/Caving

This game requires several strong able-bodied players.

How to Play: The four strongest players form a circle by placing their arms around each other's shoulders. This inner circle is strengthened by each member bracing one leg behind them for added support.

The other players then start attaching themselves to this inner circle. Each new player joins by placing an arm around the waist of the players on either side of them. They then lean into the circle with their head down and place their legs wide, with one leg behind them, similar to forming a rugby scrum. This continues until only the two lightest players remain.

The leader then tests the structure to confirm it is safe and makes sure the four members of the inner circle have tucked their heads down. Then one of the lightweight players climbs the structure while the other one goes caving by crawling between the legs of the players forming the structure.

Because of the physical nature of this game, its use may be limited with players with a physical disability. An adaptation for these players is to use caving but not climbing.

❑ Anger Ball

Players sit in a circle on the floor facing inwards with their backs straight and their legs open in a V, so that their only contact with neighbouring players is their toes.

How to Play: The players throw a soft foam ball one to the other. Each player must say what makes them angry as they throw the ball, as hard as possible, to someone else in the circle.

Variation(s): The activity can also be converted to sound essences or grunts.

Materials required: A soft foam ball ('nerf' or similar) the size of a soccer ball.

It is very difficult to maintain anger in this game. The act of "throwing one's anger" tends to release the tension that caused the anger in the first place.

❑ I Am Me

How to Play: In this game players move around the room in a movement pattern of right foot stamp, left foot stamp, two foot jump.

In each case, the hand (in the form of a clenched fist) cleaves through the air as the foot or feet make contact with the floor.

The movement pattern is linked to a sequence of three words. **I** (right foot stamp) **am** (left foot stamp) **player's name** (jump).

Variation(s): A variation is to remain seated, chanting the phrase "I am [**player's name**]."

❑ Consonant Karate

This game is similar to **I Am Me** (above).

How to Play: Individual players shape their hands as if making a 'karate chop.'

Each player then cleaves the air with their hands and stamps their feet.

While making these motions, they exhale forcefully making the sound of a 'hard' consonant — *c*, *t*, *d*, or *g*. The sounds *f*, *b* and *sh* may also be used.

Variation(s): This game can be converted to a rhythmic tribal dance by positioning the group in two well-spaced lines facing one another. These lines can then move together and apart, stamping and exhaling consonant sounds.

Care should be taken to emphasize that this is a 'non-contact' dance.

❑ Duelling With Balloons

The game begins with the players sitting in a circle with a fully-inflated balloon placed in the centre.

How to Play: The leader selects a helper who is the champion and hands that player a balloon of a different colour.

The helper (champion) then walks around the circle slowly, selecting a challenger. When the champion has chosen a challenger they proceed to hit the challenger with their balloon. Challengers can defend themselves by taking the balloon from the centre of the circle and hitting the champion with it. The fight stops when one of the players is forced to drop, or willingly drops, the balloon they are using.

Variation(s): If this game goes well, a variation is to put a deflated balloon in the centre of the circle. Now the challenger can defend themselves only after they have blown up the balloon.

Another variation is the creation of a theatrical scenario in which the protagonists are transformed into gladiators and the audience becomes spectators at a Roman amphitheatre. The spectators then shout in support of one or the other of the gladiators.

Keep a constant eye on things to make sure players do not get too rough. This game usually requires that the rules be repeated several times.

❑ Six Hammers for Mrs. Dooley

This is a follow-the-leader game.

How to Play: Players sit in a circle and must obey the commands of the leader. The hammers are parts of your body.

One and two are your hands. Three and four are your feet. Five is your head and six is your tongue. When the leader calls out a command, the players must move the part(s) of the body referred to in that command. For example, "Five hammers for Mrs. Dooley" means move both hands, both feet and your head.

When the leader mentions Mr. Dooley, e.g., "Two hammers for Mr. Dooley," the players must not move.

Materials required: Chairs.

This game must be played slowly. If it still proves too difficult for a particular group, changing the name from Mrs. Dooley to a name familiar to your area may make things easier. Simplifying, by using only four hammers, will also help, particularly when working with younger groups.

❑ Hand Jive

This game requires music with a steady, slow, rhythmic beat. Simple country dance music works well (e.g., "Merry Sherwood Rangers" or "Haste to the Wedding"). You should record the same piece of music three or four times to make it long enough to allow all players to learn a simple hand jive.

Divide the group into pairs.

57

How to Play: Seat the pairs and have each pair create a simple hand jive routine to the music. The only restrictions on the routines are that they must be consistent and repeatable.

Play the music one or two times so that the pairs are familiar with it before they start to create their routines.

Variation(s): A simpler version of this game is for the leader to teach the routine.

A more complicated version is to have Player #1 teach their partner Player #2 a routine and Player #2 teach Player #1 a routine. The two players then put their routines together and teach another pair the routine.

Materials required: Music and a tape/CD/record player.

Players with severe physical or developmental challenges may require extra assistance to be successful. This may mean extra time and/or additional help.

BODY AWARENESS, TRUST AND SENSITIVITY GAMES

The games in this section require players to place their trust in other members of the group. While it could be argued that all drama games have an element of trust involved, these games require something more, often demanding that players literally place themselves in the hands of the group.

The games in this section often involve body contact and a degree of physical intimacy that may, by and large, be missing from other games. This often demands a high degree of sensitivity on the part of the group and extra vigilance on the part of the leader. However, these activities may prove extremely beneficial experiences for the more physically insolated players of a group. Many of these games help players develop an awareness of their own body schema. As a leader it is important to help players become aware of their own and others' boundaries.

Remember, players respond differently to being touched. Careful planning, keeping the players focused on tasks, and sensitive leadership should ensure success with these activities.

□ **Hug Tag**

How to Play: One player is IT. IT holds a soft cushion in their hands, and try to place it on the tummy of other players.

All other players try to avoid being caught by hugging another player when IT tries to tag them. IT cannot tag players who are in an embrace.

Variation(s): Limiting the time for a hug, having players count out loud to three before hugging, or requiring players to introduce themselves before hugging, are all variations on this game.

❑ Blind

There are many blind games; this is probably the simplest.

How to Play: Divide the group into pairs and ask one player in each pair to shut their eyes and keep them shut for the duration of the game.

The 'seeing' player then guides their 'blind' partner around the room, preventing them from bumping into anything.

Variation(s): The leader can complicate the game by placing obstacles around the room.

The game can be modified by experimenting with the many different ways of guiding:

• using speech;
• non-verbal communication;
• body contact;
• guiding using one finger; etc.

A further variation of this game is to give the 'seeing' player four or five objects, which they pass to the 'blind' player to touch and try to recognize. The 'blind' player then holds the names of the items in their memory until the end of the exercise. At that time, the 'blind' player has to name them in the correct sequence. If it is difficult for the group, change the rule so that the player has to name two items in any order.

This game can also be followed by **Blind Tag** (below) or **Controlling the Traffic** (p. 60).

❑ Blind Tag

As in **Blind**, above, the group is divided into pairs.

How to Play: One player in each pair is the guide and the other closes their eyes and is 'blind.' A balloon is given to the blind member of one pair. That pair is now IT.

The pair on IT then chases other pairs and tries to tag the blind member of another pair with the balloon. When they are successful, the pair they tag becomes IT and must use the balloon to tag the blind member of another pair.

Materials required: Balloons.

59

The game can become hectic and may require a lot of direction. Simplify if necessary by making it legal for the pair that is IT to tag either member of the other pairs.

❑ Controlling the Traffic

How to Play: One player, who keeps their eyes closed throughout the game, is led to one end of the room. The other members of the group then place objects about the floor.

Next, ask one of the players to guide the 'blind' player across the floor from one end of the room to the other.

If necessary, the rest of the group can help guide the 'blind' player across the room.

Variation(s):   Make the process more difficult by instructing the group:

- not to touch the 'blind' player;
- to use sounds but not words to guide the 'blind' player; or
- to remain silent, guiding the 'blind' player with touch.

Materials required: Various objects.

Adjust the degree of complexity posed by the obstacles to meet the capabilities of the 'blind' player.

❑ Keeper of the Keys

How to Play: One player (the Keeper of the Keys) is blindfolded and sits in the middle of the room. At their feet is a set of keys. The other players sit in a large circle some distance away from the Keeper.

One at a time, the players creep up to the Keeper and try to steal the keys without being caught. The Keeper cannot move from their position and tries to catch players by making wide sweeps with their arms. Once caught, the thief has to return to their original place in the circle.

If anyone succeeds in stealing the keys they become the Keeper.

Variation(s):   The keeper points at where they think the thief is.

If caught, thieves freeze where they are.

The thieves are also blind.

Once the keys are stolen the thieves have to pass them on as many times as possible without the Keeper hearing where they are.

Materials required: A blindfold and a set of keys.

60

☐ Eye Am the Leader

Ask the group to work in pairs.

How to Play: Pairs take it in turns to give commands to their partner using only their eyes. They try to get them to move around the room, sit, stand, pick things up, etc.

Variation(s):   Use one eye only.
   Work in larger groups and develop a dance or movement sequence.
   Add simple noises.

☐ Walk My Walk

Ask the group to get into pairs.

How to Play: Player #1 walks as naturally as possible while Player #2, walking a few steps behind, watches.
   Player #2 then slowly moves alongside Player #1 and places a hand on #1's shoulder.
   They then walk together while #2 gets a sense of #1's rhythm. When ready, Player #2 walks ahead, copying #1's walk as closely as possible. The partners then discuss the experience and reverse roles.
   After a while, bring the pairs back together as a group and share observations and walks.

☐ Puppets and Puppeteers

Divide the group into pairs. In each pair, one player is the puppet and the other is the puppeteer.

How to Play: The puppeteer holds a thin garden cane or bamboo stick which they pretend powers their puppet's movements. When the puppeteer touches a body part with the stick, the puppet moves that body part away from the stick.
   If the shoulder is touched from behind, the puppet moves it forward. If a finger is touched from below, the puppet moves it up.

Variation(s):   As the game progresses, puppets can be asked to add sound to their movements or move quickly when touched with the stick and then slowly return to their original 'resting' position.

Materials required: Garden canes.

Care must be taken that the puppeteers do not abuse their powers.

61

❑ **Clay Modelling**

Working in pairs, one player is a clay figure and the other a sculptor.

> *How to Play:* The sculptor works with the clay (their partner's body) to create different shapes.

> *Variation(s):* A variation of this game uses groups of three or more players in which one player as the sculptor moulds the other players into tableaus showing emotions, abstract concepts, scenes from life, etc.

❑ **Mannequins**

This game is played in pairs.

> *How to Play:* One player is a mannequin or model in a shop window. The other player is a window dresser who places the mannequin in a position that advertises a particular product. The product may be chosen by the leader, the group, or each pair.

> *Variation(s):* The window dresser positions the mannequin in silence without telling them what it is the mannequin is modelling.
> Each pair works together to advertise the product.
> The mannequin is allowed to move.
> At some point, the window dressers from each pair go around and has a look at the other mannequins and tries to guess what it is they are advertising.

❑ **Chinese Puzzles**

Select a group of three players, preferably composed of one helper and two other players.

> *How to Play:* Ask the group to come into the centre of a circle of the remaining players.
> Ask one of the players to keep their eyes closed while the helper and another player form a simple shape (e.g., by holding hands side-by-side). When the shape is formed, the leader takes the 'blind' player over to it. Keeping their eyes closed, the player must then determine the positions of the other two players through feeling the shape.
> When the 'blind' player thinks they know the shape, the leader takes them away and the other two players unfold. Now comes the tricky bit. With their eyes now open, the 'blind' player attempts to put the other two players back into the same shape.

62

Variation(s): A simpler version of this game is to have two players create the shape while the third player, eyes open, watches. Having completed the shape, the pair untangles and the third player attempts to put them back into their shape.

Another, even simpler, version — one that acts as a good warm-up for **Mannequins** (above) or **Clay Modelling** (see p. 62) — is to play the above game with only two players. One creates the shape and the other watches. The watcher can then either recreate the shape, or copy the shape using their own body or the leader's body.

Reshaping the players is very difficult for anyone and almost impossible for players with spatial problems. Try to keep the shapes very simple. As leader, assist the 'blind' player by asking specific questions such as "Who is that?"; "Where are their feet?"; etc.

Once the group has the idea of the game, divide the group into threes, and let them play the game on their own. You will need to keep an eye on proceedings, particularly with adolescents.

❑ Moving Statues

This game works best with twelve players, although it can be made to work with six to sixteen. Each player in the group is going to form part of a statue.

How to Play: Begin by assigning each player a number from one to twelve.

Then have Player #2 place Player #1 in a pose (e.g., hands on hips). Player #3 then attaches Player #2 to #1, forming a new statue. Player #4 then attaches #3 to the statue.

The game continues, with each player attaching the player before them to the statue. When Player #12 has attached #11 to the statue, #1 extricates themselves from the statue and attaches #12 to the statue. Then Player #2 extricates themselves and attaches #1 again. In this way, the statue is continually changing.

This game can be very confusing and you may have to keep explaining the rules.

Players need time to attach the player before them and must be reminded to stay in the statue until it is their turn to come out.

❑ Circle Trust

Start this game with a demonstration.

How to Play: Ask one of the players to stand in the centre of a small circle of about six to eight other players and the leader. In groups where players need assistance from helpers it is best to start the demonstration using these helpers.

The player in the centre closes their eyes and stands with feet together and arms by their sides.

The circle then becomes as tight as it can. Now the members of the circle slowly and gently move the player in the centre back and forth and from side to side.

The overall effect should be similar to a blade of grass being blown by a very gentle breeze. The emphasis throughout must be on support, safety and trust.

After demonstrating how safe the circle is, ask if any players want to try being in the centre.

Note: **The first time you use this game, do not try to move the player in the centre more than an inch or two in any direction.** The amount of movement can be increased as confidence increases each time the game is played. However, movement of six inches is probably as much as anyone should be moved without frightening them.

Players with a disability are generally reluctant to relax and trust the players who are supporting them. They usually show this by moving their feet and trying to regain their balance.

❑ Lifting Trust

As with **Circle Trust**, above, it is best to begin this game with a demonstration.

How to Play: The player to be lifted lies on their back on the floor with their eyes closed and arms held loosely across their body.

The team of eight lifters stands three on either side and one each at the head and feet. On a pre-arranged signal, they lift the prone player's body above their heads and hold it there for a few seconds.

Then, keeping their feet still, they gently start to lower the body, moving it slowly from side to side as it descends. Once the player is back on the floor, they keep their eyes closed until the team of lifters has moved back from them. Then the player opens their eyes and gets up in their own time.

64

Note: It is possible that up to ten players may be needed as 'lifters' if the player to be lifted is relatively tall and/or heavy. Remember it is possible to lift anyone as long as the weight is sensibly distributed. It is very important that neither the player to be lifted nor the players doing the lifting laugh during the game, because this makes lifting more difficult and therefore more dangerous.

Be sure to show players how to get up from the floor without becoming giddy:
1. roll onto your side;
2. then roll onto your stomach;
3. use your hands to push up from the floor onto one knee; and
4. then move from your knee to a standing position.

It is important that lifters keep the lifted player's body, head and feet in as straight a line as possible, so as to avoid placing stress on their spine.

❑ Frighten Me

This game is played in pairs and requires a high level of trust.

How to Play: One player lies down on their back on the ground spread-eagled, while the other player walks around the edge of their body, gradually moving closer by stepping over hands, legs, body, head, etc.

If there is sufficient trust, the standing player might even jump and land with their feet on either side of the prone player's leg, arm, head, etc.

❑ These Are My Hands

This game can be played as a variation on **Strangers** (p. 34).

How to Play: Players move freely around the room, meeting and greeting one another.

At a given signal players stop to examine another player's hands. As they do this they describe their partner's hands, e.g., "Your hands feel very soft." In addition, players are asked to notice and comment on any jewellery their partner has on their hands, e.g., "I notice that you have a ring on your third finger." Players should be encouraged to ask their partner questions based on what they think they find out from their hands, e.g., "I notice that you have very long fingers; have you ever played the piano?"

After meeting and greeting most or all of the group, players are asked to sit down in a circle and discuss what they found out about their partner's hands.

65

Variation(s): A variation is to have all players mill around the room with their eyes closed. In this variation players explore the texture and 'qualities' of their partner's hands primarily through touch.

❑ Faces

How to Play: In this game, the players walk around the room with their eyes shut.

When players meet each other, they stop and examine each other's face with their hands. They then try to guess whose face they are touching. Having done this, they move on to new faces.

❑ Face Massage

Massage is a useful tool for relaxation, and face massage is particularly relaxing. **Face Massage** requires a high degree of trust among players and should not be attempted in early sessions with a group.

How to Play: Begin by dividing the group into pairs.

One player in each pair then lies on their back and the other kneels behind them so that their partner's head is cradled in their lap.

They then gently massage their partner's face, using the thumbs in gentle circular motions.

If your group has a large number of individuals who are physically dependent on helpers, it is a good idea to organize training sessions for the helpers so that they can practice massage on each other before working with their physically-dependent partners.

❑ Group Back Massage

How to Play: Begin by having the players sit in a tight circle, each player facing the next player's back.

Each player then massages the shoulders and neck of the player in front of them.

After a few minutes, have the players flop onto the player in front of them and focus on breathing.

❑ Relaxation

It is valuable to include time to relax in all drama game sessions, especially if you are running regular game sessions. There are many ways of getting players to relax — this is a simple one.

How to Play: Ask the players to lie on their backs on the floor. Then, using a slow and soothing voice tell them to let each part of their body relax into the floor. Start with the feet and work through the legs to the body and head until the players are completely relaxed. Try to get each player to relax their entire body.

Soothing music can assist players in relaxing. You can check if a player is relaxed by seeing if their foot is loose when you gently pick it up.

It is possible you may have to spend time waking players up at the end of this game.

IMPROVISATIONAL AND MIME GAMES

In some ways all of the games in this section are problem-solving exercises. As such they demand a degree of imagination and abstract thinking not present in many of the other games.

For some groups you may need to build in stages from 'concrete operations' (games where there is a specific answer) to more 'imaginative' games which allow the group to 'invent' their own answer to the problem.

Also, contrary to popular opinion, not everyone can do mime. It is believed that there is a readiness for mime just as there is for reading, talking, etc. For some players who have difficulty transferring ideas from one event to another, or from one context to another, it is best to start by miming events that are very familiar to the players. Miming abstract or unfamiliar actions or events may be setting the players up for failure.

❏ Idols

Divide the group into pairs. In each pair, one player stands in front of the other, both facing the same direction.

How to Play: The player in front (#1) puts their hands behind their back. The other player (#2) puts their arms under #1's armpits. In this way, #2 becomes #1's hands.

They now walk around the room meeting other pairs with the #1s doing the talking and the #2s performing the hand actions. After a while, reverse the roles.

This is a great game for confusion.

❏ Mirror Work

Divide the group into pairs and ask the players in each pair to face one another.

How to Play: One player in each pair becomes a mirror and the other player 'uses' the mirror. The mirror must attempt to recreate the actions of the player using it.

67

Have the players using the mirrors begin with simple tasks like brushing their teeth or combing their hair.

After a couple of actions, have the players switch roles.

As the game progresses, allow each pair to decide which tasks must be mirrored by their partners.

This game can cause problems for players who have difficulty conceptualizing space. However, it usually goes well as long as you emphasize the need to perform the actions slowly and clearly.

❑ Chinese Mime

This is a mime version of **Chinese Whispers** (see p. 50).

How to Play: The group sits in a circle, facing outwards, preferably with eyes closed.

The first player goes into the centre of the circle. The second player only is allowed to turn around to watch the first perform a short mime.

The first player sits down. At this point, the third player is told to open their eyes and the second player repeats the mime as accurately as possible for the third player.

Players must repeat everything they see in the performance (even the mistakes). When they have done the mime they are allowed to watch others performing.

The mime usually changes each time it is performed and may be quite unidentifiable by the end. The first player should repeat their original mime once everyone has finished.

Variation(s): Add noises to the mime.
Work in pairs.

❑ Exaggerate My Walk

How to Play: Players form a large circle. One at a time, players walk around inside the circle.

Each player exaggerates the walk of the player who went before them.

Variation(s): In a variation, the leader starts walking around the inside of the circle. After one revolution the player on their left (#1) joins in walking behind the leader. It is this player's job to change the leader's walk. After another revolution, the leader returns to the circle. The next player on the left (#2) then enters the circle. Walking behind #1, #2 exaggerates #1's walk. This continues until all the players have had a turn.

Once a group has the general idea, suggest making only subtle changes to walks. Exaggerated walks can be used to create clown characters and then clown scenes (see **Clown Fights** below).

❑ Clown Fights

How to Play: Begin by dividing the group into pairs.

The players in each pair face one another. One player initiates an action, the other responds. Each takes turns at both giving and receiving an action.

Pairs then explore the actions and responses suggested by the leader to develop a 'Clown Fight' vocabulary.

Actions and their Responses include:
- slow blow, fast response;
- fast blow, delayed response;
- fast blow, response in different part of body;
- fast blow, felt by aggressor;
- fast blow, felt by both players; or
- any variations.

Once the basic movements and commands have been learned, players can piece together a three- to ten-minute clown scene.

This game demands that the players concentrate and that the leader uses extreme caution.

Timing is very important and the players must understand that they are only touching each other, not hitting each other. At the first sign of too much aggression, the leader must re-establish control.

❑ Hats

Bring in an assortment of hats; each hat suggests a different character.

How to Play: Let players try the hats on.

Ask the players to imagine what sort of person might wear each hat.

Ask players to put on their hat and imagine they are the person who owns that hat.

Then get players to greet each other in their hats.

Variation(s):   Players exchange hats, thus changing characters.

Create scenes in which characters meet.

Create unlikely meetings (places, situations).

69

❑ The Clothesline

This is an adaptation of an exercise originally developed by Charles Marowitz for work on Shakespearean texts. It was intended to help actors understand the rhythm of unfamiliar lines, and to identify proper breathing pauses within the lines which do not work contrary to the sense, or rhythm, of the lines.

> *How to Play:* The group stands or sits in a circle. The group leader chooses an unfamiliar sentence which none-theless matches the group's capabilities; e.g., for intellectually 'able' individuals this would usually mean using a few lines from Shakespeare such as:
>
> "Life's but a walking shadow, a poor player
> That struts and frets his hour upon the stage
> And then is heard no more: It is a tale
> Told by an idiot, full of sound and fury,
> Signifying nothing."
> [*Macbeth*, Act V, Scene V]
>
> The group then speaks the sentence, including the punctuation, one word at a time. Initially, each member of the group speaks only one word, or punctuation mark.
>
> Then each individual takes one word only, but instead of speaking the punctuation this time a breathing pause is observed in its place: a period being a full breath, a semi-colon = a half breath, a comma = a quarter breath, etc.
>
> Slowly the group builds the 'sense' and rhythm of the chosen sentence until the group is able to speak the sentence as if speaking with one voice.

Variation(s):
- having the group speak the sentence as a chorus; and
- clapping/stamping the rhythm of the sentence.

❑ Sing the Punctuation

Players are given, or bring to the group, a line(s) from well-known songs, poems or similar writings.

> *How to Play:* Ask the group to find a partner. Every player 'chooses' their own line which they use throughout the game. It is helpful if this line is different from their partner's line.
>
> Working in pairs, individuals converse using this one line.
>
> First ask them to speak the line including the punctuation as 'flatly' as possible.

Then assign conflicting emotions, e.g., happy/sad, where one partner says their line 'sadly' while the other says it 'happily.'

Then ask the pairs to try to apply an operatic 'song-spiel' to the line, giving a sing-song, though not always musical, quality.

Finally, ask the pairs to give their lines what they feel is 'correct' emotional emphasis.

❏ **Speak the Sub-Text**

How to Play: This exercise can be approached in two basic ways:

1. Two players are asked to converse. At any point, a player may be asked to 'annotate' their dialogue by following each statement with a comment on:
   a) the player's own feeling;
   b) what the player is trying to get the other player to do or say; or
   c) what the player thought the other player's last sentence meant.

2. Players are divided into groups of four, and each group of four is divided into two teams of two (A&B and C&D). Player A speaks to Player C while Player B stands behind Player A and Player D stands behind Player C. After each sentence spoken by Player A, Player B comments on:
   a) what they think Player A's sentence really meant;
   b) what they think Player A is trying to get Player C to do or say; or
   c) Player A's feelings.
   Player D does the same for Player C.

This exercise can be very effective when coupled with techniques of **role reversal**, i.e., replaying a scene with each player taking the other's original part. This helps individuals to view the scene from a different perspective, and possibly gain insight into the other player's position.

It is advisable to begin the game as a demonstration with all other participants acting as the audience.

B's and D's roles are particularly difficult for inhibited players if used early in the life of the group.

❏ **I'm Sorry, I Must Be Leaving**

How to Play: One player starts an action and a second player joins in the scene.

71

When a third player joins the other two, the first player in the scene must leave. This third player can join the scene at any time.

The game is played with dialogue but all actions are mimed. The four basic rules of the game are:

1. there must be no more than two players on stage at any given time;
2. when it is your turn to leave, you must find a suitable excuse for doing so;
3. the new performer in the scene has the right to change the actions; and
4. individuals can come in and join the scene whenever and as often as they wish.

For example, Player #1 starts the scene by pretending to wash a car. Player #2 enters and asks #1 to help trim a hedge, and #1 agrees and pretends to trim the hedge.

When #3, pretending to be a dentist, enters and asks who is the next patient, #2 becomes the patient and #1 leaves with some excuse like "I'm sorry, I must be leaving. I hear the phone ringing."

❏ One-Line Stands

Split the group into pairs. Each pair labels themselves A and B.

How to Play: Player A is given the opening line of a conversation. Player B has to reply immediately. Then the partners continue to take turns speaking (A then B then A and so on) until a suitable conclusion is reached. (This will take longer for some pairs than others.)

There should be no prior discussion about the roles of the speakers or the setting — these should become clear during the conversation.

When everyone is finished, B is given the next opening line.

Variation(s): Try, as ever, to fit the material to the needs and capabilities of you group.

Give partners the closing line of a conversation. Each has to try to 'slip' their closing line into the conversation as smoothly as possible.

You can ask some of the pairs to show their improvisations afterwards. It is interesting to see the variety of scenes suggested by the same line.

Some groups may like to be given more facts about their characters and the setting before they start.

❑ Cocktail Party

Two players are invited to participate in a cocktail party, office party or similar social gathering.

How to Play: Each is asked to choose, or is given by the group, a topic which they are to converse on. They are then instructed to speak to the other person as if they were at a cocktail party, with neither listening to their partner's conversation. Each must try to appear as if they are listening but must in fact be thinking about and/or rehearsing their next line. The effect should be two totally unconnected monologues.

Variation(s): This game can be varied in a number of ways:

- Each speaker should try to make it appear as if they heard their partner by, immediately prior to launching in to their own unconnected topic, repeating, word for word, the last phrase that their partner said.
- Each player's status can be altered during the conversation, allowing one or other of the players to control the conversation. A third player can be introduced who may dominate both conversations or be totally ignored by both parties or some other variation.
- Emotional quality can be added to the conversation by adding some background 'given circumstances,' e.g., one player hates/wishes to date/is married to/is the employee of the other.
- In fact there are many different possibilities. Choices should always be made on the basis of the needs of the participants.

❑ Yes/No Interrogation

Two players sit facing each other in the centre of the circle. One is the 'interrogator,' the other is the 'suspect,' behind whom stands an 'executioner' with a balloon in their hand.

How to Play: The interrogator asks the suspect questions. If the 'suspect' hesitates or says yes or no, the executioner hits them over the head with the balloon.

Variation(s): You can vary this game by having an additional executioner behind the interrogator. I suggest you give some thought to who plays what role. Nevertheless, most groups seem to like the slapstick element of the game.

Materials required: Balloons.

❑ **Nursery Rhyme Thump**

This is similar to **Yes/No Interrogation**, above.

How to Play: In this game, however, the suspect has to recite a nursery rhyme without hesitating or making a mistake. The price for either is being hit over the head with a balloon.

Materials required: Balloons.

Once again careful choices need to be made concerning who plays what role.

❑ **I'm Taking Charge**

The scene is an office in a small company. In the scene, there are three performers: a senior administrator, a manager, and a 'gofer'.

How to Play: The senior administrator has a large balloon and the manager has a small balloon. The gofer has no balloon.

The essence of the scene is that the administrator must make a constant stream of unreasonable requests to the manager, hitting them over the head with the balloon as they do so.

The manager must use their balloon to convey the administrator's requests to the gofer. The gofer must find a way to comply with the requests.

This chain of command continues until the leader informs them that the company's shareholders have announced a shake-up in personnel. The manager is fired and the gofer and the administrator switch positions in the company. The new administrator chooses a new manager from the audience of the other players and the whole zany experience continues.

STORYTELLING AND STORY-MAKING GAMES

Making, telling, and playing with stories leads players from the realm of games into play. Consequently, this section is set out slightly differently from the preceding game sections.

Below, you will find games and game-like structures with which to play with stories. As already mentioned storytelling and storymaking games and structures are a very good starting point for moving from drama games into extended drama work and theatre.

74

Story: A basic structure

Like games all stories have a beginning, a middle and an end. A story, unlike real life, is not necessarily bound by real time, real behaviour, physical constraints, etc.

All stories need some form of introduction in which they establish a sense of:

- **Place** (**Where** things are happening);
- **Time** (**When** the action is occurring); and
- **Character** (**Who** is involved in the story).

As the story is told the plot unfolds and there is a development of characters. During this part of the telling the audience gains a deeper and richer sense of the **Who**, **What**, and **Where** of the story. They also learn either directly or indirectly **How** and **Why** events take place.

As the story unfolds, tension builds. These tensions result in dramatic moments (entanglements or conflicts) which need to be resolved. Usually tension is created as result of conflicts between characters but may also be created by atmosphere, e.g., the reaction of a character to the environment, or even through conflicts within a single character, e.g., Hamlet.

In most successful stories there is a final dramatic moment, a climax in which all entanglements and/or conflicts come together. In complicated or intricate stories there may be many dramatic moments and even more than one climax. A climax provides the opportunity for a final resolution ('denouement'). This makes it possible that "they all live happily ever after...".

However, stories do not always have to be resolved, but may instead opt for a suspended ending in which either the ending is left in doubt or else left for the reader or listener to decide. This is used a lot by movie directors who may want to film a sequel to a blockbuster hit! It is also a technique used in Drama in Education (e.g., David Booth's work in Story drama) and Theatre for Young Audiences (e.g., Brian Way's work in Participatory Theatre) to enable the audience to physically participate in and resolve the story.

Choosing a story to tell

Selecting a theme suitable to a particular audience rests heavily on a storyteller's choice concerning the type(s) of conflicts to be resolved. Metaphorically speaking, the clothes must 'fit' the person for whom they are intended.

There are many types of story. For example:

- **Folk Tale**: Any form of narrative, written or oral, that has been handed down through the years — e.g., legends, myths and folksong.
- **Myth**: Any story that tells of origins, explains natural or social phenomena or suggests the destiny of humans through interaction of people and supernatural beings.
- **Legend**: Literally, something to be read. Usually involves a myth in which the protagonist is a person rather than a supernatural being.
- **Everyday Stories**: Spoken or written (in history books, newspapers or magazines) tales that tell the 'social history' of a particular community at a particular point in time.
- **Personal Narrative**: A story from the teller's own life.

The essence of storytelling

Storytellers take their audience (listener and/or viewer) on a journey. The successful storyteller must clearly establish **Who** is involved in the story and **Where** and **When** the story takes place. Also, the storyteller has to establish that anything can happen (particularly important if the tale involves fantasy or magic). As the story unfolds the storyteller must let their audience know **What** is happening.

The essence of storytelling is to create large scale 'fibs' in such a way that it draws the audience in, touches them emotionally and makes them believe, at least for the duration of the story, that what they are hearing is true.

What follows are several games and game-like structures to help you make, tell and play with stories.

Personal Narratives

Everyone has a story to tell about their lives. Personal narratives are storytelling structures that allow every player the opportunity to talk about something they know well.

Tell players they should only share what they feel comfortable telling the group. They can share as much or as little detail as they want.

Some people are more able to express themselves than others. Allow adequate time and appropriate help for those people who need it.

On the other hand, if the players in your group are very talkative, it is often helpful to set a time limit. This will have to be determined by the size of your group and the amount of time available for your session.

All the following storytelling games using personal narratives are played sitting in a circle.

The following are good starting points for personal stories.

76

❏ **This is My Name**

How to Play: In this game, each member of the group is asked to speak about their name. They can say as little or as much as desired about the origins of their name, its meaning, their family, whether they like the name, what name they would like to be called instead, etc.

This is a non-directive open-ended game. The player speaking decides how much and how deep to make their comments, based on how comfortable they feel about talking to the group on a personal level.

This is an illustration of **spotlighting** — providing the opportunity for an individual to be centre stage for as long as they feel comfortable. It also provides a platform for self-expression. Often a great deal of information is gathered through the use of this simple spotlighting technique.

❏ **How I Got Up This Morning**

How to Play: Ask each player to talk about how they got out of the house. Ask them to describe the sequence of events from the time they awoke to the time they finished their breakfast or left the house.

❏ **What I Saw On My Way To...**

How to Play: Ask each player to talk about what they saw on the journey from their house on their way to your session.

❏ **My Favourite...**

How to Play: Ask each player to talk about something they really like. The topics are almost endless but examples might be:
● my favourite holiday;
● my favourite meal;
● my best friend; etc.

❏ **Where I Play(ed) as a Child**

How to Play: Ask each player to talk about where and what they played as a young child. Also ask them who they played these activities with.

❏ **I Remember When...**

How to Play: Ask each player to talk about a particular time in their life. For example:

- their earliest memory; or
- their first day at school.

❏ **The Most Incredible Thing That Ever Happened to Me...**

How to Play: Ask each player to talk about the most incredible thing that has happened in their lives. It could be a strange occurrence, a chance meeting with a celebrity or anything they consider incredible.

Variation(s):   A variation is to play this game with the players working in pairs. Each player must tell the other the most incredible thing that ever happened to them; however, the story they tell must be a complete lie.

After each pair has finished their stories the group once more forms a circle. Each pair retells their story to the group — however, partner A tells partner B's story and vice-versa.

Story-Making: Creating Improvised Stories

Below are presented several different ways of using games to create stories.

❏ **Word Tennis**

This game is played in pairs.

How to Play: Each pair finds a space and stands a good distance apart facing each other.

The partners create stories one word at a time, taking turns to add a new word to the sentence. Each word is 'hit' to the other partner across the space between them. The game is played somewhat like a tennis match with the words as invisible balls.

Variation(s):   As a variation, do not attempt to make 'sense' of the story — the effect is more like 'free-form' poetry than story-telling.

❏ **Story Circles**

The group sits in a circle.

How to Play: In this game the group collaboratively creates a story. The leader starts the story. The person on the leader's right then adds a sentence to the story. This continues all the way around the circle with each member of the group adding a sentence to the story.

The story continues until the group brings it to a conclusion.

Variation(s): A variation is for the leader to stop the story at a particular point, e.g., after everyone has added a sentence. At this point the leader asks each member of the group to tell the other players their own conclusion to the story.

❑ Who? Where? When?

The group sits in a circle.

How to Play: The leader asks the group to suggest only the beginning of a story by describing **Who** the story is about, and **Where** and **When** the story is to take place.

Once these basic elements have been agreed upon, as in **Circle Stories**, each member of the group adds a sentence to the story.

Variation(s): A variation is for the group to work in threes. In this variation, each of the three players is assigned one part of the Introduction, i.e.:

- player A says **who** the story is about;
- player B tells **where** the story takes place; and
- player C says **when** the story takes place.

Once these essential elements have been agreed upon, the trio tells the story with each player adding one sentence at a time.

Allow time for three tales to be started, as this allows each of the three players to say **Who** one of the three tales is about.

If it is appropriate for your group, ask each member of the group to tell the rest of the group one of the three tales their trio created.

❑ In the Style Of...

This is a variation on **Who? Where? When?** (above).

How to Play: In this game the group suggests what type of story the group or the trios are to tell. For example, the group having decided on Who? Where? When? may decide that the story must be a Murder Mystery. Other examples might include: a Romance Tale, a Fairy Tale, a Ghost Story, a Hero/Heroine adventure, or even a story in the style of a famous author like Stephen King, J.R.R. Tolkein, Beatrix Potter, etc.

79

❏ Story Mime

How to Play: The group sits in a circle with one of the players standing in the centre.

The other players have to compose a story by having each player add a line. As the story unfolds, the player in the centre of the circle has to act it out.

This game may be difficult for players with limited verbal skills or players with limited imaginations. They will need time and positive support.

Players should be allowed to pass if they can't think of a line to add.

The leader can also assist by suggesting possible story lines.

Playing With Written Stories

If the individuals in your group are able to read, written sources abound for you to explore in dramatic ways. Plays, novels, short stories, picture books, magazines and newspapers all offer wonderful possibilities for dramatic play using the basic principles already explored with the group through drama games. A few suggestions are made below concerning how to help your group to 'Play with Text(s).'

❏ Living Newspaper: Playing With Everyday Stories

Newspapers provide a valuable and re-usable source for dramatic play. Everyday there are new stories that your group can use. Working with a newspaper means taking a step forward from your work in drama games. However, by applying the basic approach already presented and the few basic principles identified below, newspapers can provide a very valuable resource for your group.

This works best when small groups of four to six people work together.

How to Play: Ask each small group to follow these steps:
- Individually read several stories in the newspaper.
- Read and share stories with other players.
- Select a story to work with and explore.
- As a group, look at the structure of the story. Identify:
  - **What** is happening in the story (the basic facts)?
  - **Who** is involved in the story?
  - **Where** does the action take place?
  - **When** does this happen?

Once the basic facts of the story have been determined, the group can decide how they want to play with the story.

To do this it is good to discuss **Why** the events in the story happened.

Here are some simple ways to play with the story:

- Retell or act out the story, keeping as close to the original facts as possible.
- Each player tells a different section of the story.
- Each player becomes one of the characters in the story.
- One player is the narrator while the others are a chorus. The chorus can act like a 'colour commentator':
  - providing background sounds to 'animate' the story; or
  - acting as 'onlookers' reacting to the events of the tale.
- Retell the story from a particular perspective:
  - from the point of view of one of the characters; or
  - by a journalist recreating the events.

In telling the tale there are many different dramatic techniques that you might consider using. For example:

- players speak about themselves in the third person;
- players speak to themselves (soliloquy, monologues) or to the audience (asides, commentary);
- same role played by more than one player;
- use more than one language;
- play scene in past and future as well as present; and/or
- use song(s).

Use a combination of any of these (or other) techniques. Also, encourage groups to:

- try to keep things simple;
- build the story slowly in stages, one step at a time;
- remember not to lose the story in the action; and
- choose actions that help them to tell the story.

Make sure you allow time for each group to work on their stories before they present them.

Ask each group if they would like to present their story to the rest of the group. This should be a choice for each group to make.

After all the presentations you can allow time for the players to discuss their work. If it is appropriate you can provide time for the groups to *revise* their work in light of the discussion.

Variation(s): Once your group is comfortable with this approach, you may want to try some of the following variations:

- invite comments from the 'audience';
- invite the audience to direct the action; and/or
- invite the audience to play your role.

Once your group is comfortable working with newspaper stories you may want to move to more difficult written stories (see **Speak the Speech I Pray You**, below).

❑ **Speak the Speech I Pray You**

Working with Play Scripts: When trying to introduce working with play texts as sources for storytelling and storymaking, I like to begin with scenes from some of Shakespeare's famous plays.

Beginning with Shakespeare can be quite intimidating because many people are afraid of Shakespeare's language, particularly his verse. However it is *because* of the richness and unfamiliarity of the language that there is such a wealth of possibilities for dramatic play!

What follows are some simple playful approaches that can make Shakespeare's texts 'user-friendly.' These same techniques can be used with any play script, but are particularly useful when working with plays written a long time ago or in verse.

Remember that a play script, whether it is by a modern writer or by William Shakespeare, tells a tale.

It is always best to start with a play that you know well. Start with a section of text that contains a lot of action, e.g., the last scene of *Hamlet* (Act V, Scene II, from the beginning of Hamlet's duel with Laertes to just before Fortinbras' entrance).

1. **Read the Scene Aloud**
   - *Each player* reads *one line*.
   - *Each player* reads *one line* (reading all punctuation and stage directions aloud).
   - *Each player* reads *one 'thought'* (Punctuation provides the speaker with clues as to where one thought begins and another one ends. See **The Clothesline** on page 70.).

2. **Perform the Scene**
   - be as true to the text as possible;
   - no dialogue — just action; and
   - play the 'sense' of the scene (no scripts).

3. **Analyze the Scene**
   - Frame-by-frame: where are the 'turning points' in the scene?
   - Use tableau(x) for each significant moment, e.g., start and finish of scene.
   - Each character says one 'quintessential' line.
   - Each character, or one chosen character, gives monologue.

4. **Report the Scene**
   - Use a narrator.
   - Newscaster interviewing scene's characters:
     - at points during scene (using 'freeze');
     - as they enter and/or leave scene;
     - using question and answer with/without studio audience;
     - as if on *Geraldo* or *Oprah*; or
     - as if a 'town hall' meeting.

5. **Replay the Scene**
   - in modern language and/or modern setting;
   - as if a major sporting event — with sports announcer (use instant replay/slow motion replay/colour commentator);
   - one person playing all the characters;
   - one person talks about themselves after the scene; or
   - as if a 30-second news item.

The techniques and approaches described above can be applied to almost any written story.

FURTHER READING

Note: Entries marked with a star (*) indicates those containing practical activities (games, ideas, exercises, etc.).

Booth, D. (1994). *Story Drama*. Markham, Ontario: Pembrook.*

Brandes, D. and Phillips, H. (1977). *Gamester's Handbook*. London, UK: Hutchinson.*

Brandes, D. (1982). *Gamester's Handbook 2*. London, UK: Hutchinson.*

Courtney, R. (1980). *The Dramatic Curriculum*. London, UK: Heinemann.

Exley, H. (ed.). (1981). *What It's Like to Be Me*. Watford, UK: Exley.

Jennings, S. (1973) *Remedial Drama*. London, UK: Pitman.*

————. (1986). *Creative Drama in Group Work*. London, UK: Winslow Press.*

Johnstone, K. (1981). *Impro — Improvisation and the Theatre*. London, UK: Eyre Metheun.*

Koste, V.G. (1994). *Dramatic Play in Childhood: Rehearsal for Life*. New York: Heinemann.

Levete, G. (1982). *No Handicap to Dance (Human Horizons Series)*. London, UK: Souvenir Press; Cambridge, MA: Brookline Books, Inc.*

McClintock, A.B. (1984). *Drama for Mentally Handicapped Children (Human Horizons Series)*. London: Souvenir Press.*

Peter, M. (1994). *Drama for All*. London, UK: David Fulton Publishers.*

Sherborne, V. (1990). *Developmental Movement for Children*. Cambridge, MA: Cambridge University Press.*

Tomlinson, R. (1984). *Disability, Theatre and Education*. Bloomington, IN: Indiana University Press.

Warren, B. (ed.). (1993). *Using Creative Arts in Therapy*, 2nd Edition. London, UK: Routledge.*

Warren, B. (ed.). (1995). *Creating a Theatre in Your Classroom*. North York, ON: Captus University Publications.*

Way, B. (1969). *Development Through Drama*. London, UK: Longmans.*

————. (1981). *Audience Participation: Theatre For Young People*. Boston, MA: Walter H. Baker.

84

AGMV
MARQUIS
Québec, Canada
1999